Vitamin K2

Vitamin K2

The Missing Nutrient for Heart and Bone Health

Dennis Goodman, MD

authorHOUSE®

AuthorHouse™
1663 Liberty Drive
Bloomington, IN 47403
www.authorhouse.com
Phone: 1 (800) 839-8640

Published by AuthorHouse 03/16/2015

ISBN: 978-1-4969-7087-9 (sc)
ISBN: 978-1-4969-7086-2 (e)

Library of Congress Control Number: 2015902515

Contents

Dedicated to Tanya, Adam, Anat, Jonathan, Rebecca, and Roselyn

Foreword

In light of the amazing medical advances made over the last 100 years, one would think we would be a healthier world. In truth, we are living shorter, less healthy lives. While these developments enable doctors to treat diseases and prolong life, most have been created in response to the needs of a population that finds itself growing sicker with each generation.

The advances themselves are godsends; what we need to address is why we are more ill, and how can we stop this sad and disheartening trend.

Part of the issue is that our food no longer nourishes us. Due to overuse of pesticides, soils are deplete of their nutrients. Then any remaining traces of nutritional value are eliminated by processing, manufacturing, and preservatives. So while grocery store shelves are packed with food, we continue to grow less nourished.

One of the reasons I was excited to contribute the Foreword to Dr. Goodman's beautiful book is that here we have an allopathic medical practitioner who embraces prevention as a key to attaining health. He recognizes the necessity of life-saving medical procedures, but embodies the belief that one of the first responsibilities of the medical community is to help patients establish lifestyles that give them an opportunity to avoid needing those procedures. One important way to do that is to truly examine our diets, physical activity, and stress levels. At the apex of that triangle is making sure we are getting the valuable vitamins and minerals that allow our bodies to operate optimally.

This is just one front where Dr. Goodman and I are likeminded: He and I share the belief that a key nutrient void from most diets that truly have an impact on our global health care crisis is Vitamin K2. Another commonality is that we have separately reached this conclusion by placing the highest possible value on science – that weighing the hypotheses that have already been posed and sifting through mountains of research can not only provide answers, but can lead you to ask the next important question. Further, we share a similar view on education – that it is a great endeavor (and accomplishment) to share knowledge in a way that is accessible for all.

The International Science and Health Foundation is a scientific community independent of business commitments whose activities are based on four main pillars – Innovation, Knowledge, Responsibility, and Cooperation – and are intended to foster a healthy point of view that benefits society. Our mission is to improve the quality of life by providing proper knowledge and supporting the development of science.

The Foundation seeks to attain our socially and economically useful objectives through:

- Initiation, promotion, and support of research programs and educational information

- Organization and funding of conferences, lectures, and readings with the participation of representatives of science, including the health and natural medicine

- Journalistic activities and information through publishing books, magazines, and brochures

- Organization of trade fairs, and co-organizing and assistance to educational institutions; and running educational web services

That is why we decided to develop our most recent education portal: VitaminK2.org. The Foundation was already impressed with the body of research substantiating Vitamin K2's bone benefits, the early evidence of its cardiovascular benefits, as well as its potential to help child populations.

But the verdict was undeniable when I heard a presentation of a study recently published in *Thrombosis and Haemostasis:* The results of this 3-year clinical trial showed Vitamin K2 actually *improved* arterial flexibility. What an amazing development!

Further, Vitamink2.org is intended to be a resource for all – consumers and medical professionals alike. Every visitor has access to the latest information pertaining to Vitamin K2, from research and analysis, to ideas about attaining a healthy lifestyle.

Inspired by passionate people who share a desire to explore new developments in the fields of health and science, the International Science and Health Foundation appreciates Dr. Goodman's accomplishment of crafting a book that carefully presents the latest and most pertinent research for the betterment of mankind.

Katarzyna Maresz, PhD
President, International Science and Health Foundation
Krakow, Poland

Introduction

In my line of work, I am bombarded with research. It could be a sales call from a pharmaceutical rep, the latest reputable scientific journal to land on my desk, or a health care seminar I am attending. I make it a personal goal to research all this material, so I can recommend the right supplements to my patients.

When my friend, an integrative general practitioner, asked if I was recommending Vitamin K2 to my patients, I was surprised. What is Vitamin K2? I decided to find out. I was shocked—and excited—at how much good research supported this nutrient for bone and heart health.

How is it possible that I had missed out, you ask? It takes time—and, more accurately, money—to get research published supporting any aspect of human health. It doesn't help that the richest food source of Vitamin K2 is a fermented soybean dish called *natto* that is enjoyed almost exclusively in certain parts of Japan. To say natto is an acquired taste is a severe understatement.

Although Vitamin K2 is a relative new comer to the supplement arena, I believe there is now enough scientific evidence to make you take notice and add it to your list of essential nutrients. A multitude of studies have been conducted proving Vitamin K2's effectiveness in three categories: **cardiovascular health, bone health, and children's health**. And more research is being done every day to support its benefits in these crucial areas to the general population.

What got my attention was a recently published study showing that Vitamin K2 supplementation reduced arterial stiffness in healthy post-menopausal women.[1] Arterial stiffness is associated with aging and atherosclerosis. This exciting study suggests that Vitamin K2 may be able to reverse the adverse effects of early atherosclerosis and aging on blood vessels. And I am sure that further studies in men and other populations will be forthcoming.

Consider the following:

- Cardiovascular disease is the No. 1 killer of men and women in America, according to the Centers for Disease Control and Prevention (CDC).[1] And with our terrible diets and lack of mobility, that ranking should hold.

- Bone health is an unseen and understated source of misery for Americans: each year, an estimated 1.5 million Americans suffer a bone fracture because of bone disease, according to the Office of the Surgeon General. In 2010, the CDC reported that there were 258,000 hospital admissions for hip fractures among people aged 65 and older. One out of five hip fracture patients die within a year of their injury.[2]

- And as you will read in this book, many health issues endured in adulthood can be diminished or even prevented if the right nutritional choices are made in childhood. And that goes *double* for bone health. We attain approximately 90 percent of our peak bone mass by the time we are 18 or 19 years old.[3]

So why is Vitamin K2 so valuable? Very simply put, Vitamin K2 is the body's light switch. It activates or "turns on" important proteins in the body such as osteocalcin for strong bones and the matrix Gla protein (MGP), which keeps calcium—that crucial bone-building nutrient—away from your arteries so they don't harden and lead to cardiovascular disease. That makes Vitamin K2 something that should be taken as a complement to vitamin D, calcium, magnesium, and other well-established dietary nutrients. And you don't have to worry about the possible side effects that come with pharmaceuticals.

This, however, is only the beginning. In *Vitamin K2: The Missing Nutrient for Heart and Bone Health*, I want to tell you why Vitamin K2 should be in your medicine cabinet next to other well-researched products like fish oil, vitamin D, and magnesium. So, I will break down how Vitamin K2 aids in the aforementioned three major health areas, the relevant research, and why supplementation is the best option for all ages.

I always urge my patients to talk to me when they come in for a visit. That spirit lies behind this book. Not only is each chapter's title a question, *Vitamin K2: The Missing Nutrient for Heart and Bone Health* is presented as a conversation between you and me: doctor and patient. Throughout the book, you will also encounter nuggets of information that complement our conversation called "Healthy Hints", and each chapter concludes with a list of takeaways called "Doctor's In(Sights)."

I will provide information in a clear, concise way while also providing the opportunity to dig deeper into Vitamin K2's assets. Or you can simply go to whatever subject—or question—that matters most to you. There is no wrong way to read this book as long as you *learn* something and put those lessons into practice.

Once you have finished *Vitamin K2: The Missing Nutrient for Heart and Bone Health*, I am confident you will share my excitement. Let's get started.

Dr. Dennis Goodman
New York, NY

Chapter 1

————◄O►————

What is Vitamin K2?

"Dr. Goodman, I recently went to the health food store with a friend who takes Vitamin D. I was curious about what I should take. After a conversation with the salesman, I was told I should be taking a bunch of supplements, including Vitamin K2 for my bones and heart. I'm so confused. Should I be taking Vitamin K2?"

Vitamin K2 is part of the Vitamin K family, a group of fat-soluble vitamins. (That means they are stored in the gastrointestinal tract and delivered to body in fat globules called chylomicrons.) You have probably heard of Vitamin K, which is crucial for the production of proteins that we need for coagulation, or blood clotting. Without Vitamin K, we would not stop bleeding. That connection was discovered in 1929, and it earned Henrik Dam and Edward Doisy the Nobel Prize in 1943.

Vitamin K is split into two groups: Vitamin K1 and Vitamin K2. The difference lies on a molecular level. Vitamin K1 has one molecule, so it is a **phylloquinone**. The K2 group has multiple molecules and known as **menaquinones**.

Members of the Vitamin K family—Vitamins K1 and K2—are similar in structure, in that they share a "quinone" ring. How they differ is in the length and degree of saturation of the carbon tail.

The Vitamin K2 group has *multiple* carbon-hydrogen atoms in its side-chain called isoprenoid residues.[1] This "side-chain" is represented in the

1

compound's name. For example, Vitamin K2 with seven isoprenoid units is known as MK-7. The "M" stands for menaquinone and "K", of course, signifies Vitamin K2.[2] So the difference between Vitamins K1 and K2 lies in the side-chains—in the length and degree of saturation of the carbon tail.

Healthy Hints:

Vitamin K2: The Basics

- Vitamin K2 is a fat-soluble substance.

- Vitamin K2 can render special proteins (vitamin K-dependent proteins) functional by the addition of carboxyl (-COOH) groups.

- Vitamin K2 is needed for normal blood coagulation (in German and Nordic languages it is "Koagulation," which is where the "K" originated).

- Vitamin K2 is made by bacteria, which give fermented foods like cheese and the Japanese natto (fermented soybeans) a high Vitamin K2 content.

- Vitamin K2 is also involved in bone formation and repair.

- Vitamin K2 is associated with reduced risk for heart disease and hip fractures.

- Vitamin K2 has been shown to inhibit calcium deposits (i.e., calcification) in blood vessels and even improve arterial flexibility.

Is all Vitamin K2 the same?

The length of the side-chain dictates Vitamin K2's ability to reach different tissues within the body. The longer the side-chain, the more effective the form of Vitamin K.[2] It will be absorbed better, stay in the blood longer, and will be more active in bone, tissues, and arteries. Vitamin K2 as MK-7 is often described as having a long half-life, which means it will be available to the body for a longer period of time.

Thirty years of studies at the University of Maastricht (the Netherlands), the leaders in vitamin K research, *have consistently shown* that Vitamin K2 in the MK-7 form is superior.

Vitamin K1 is a key ingredient in baby formula, but it will not deliver the heart-friendly and bone-health benefits that Vitamin K2 does, which I will discuss later. While these nutrients belong to the same family, they provide very different benefits.

Can I get Vitamin K2 through a healthy diet?

Probably not, unless you live in Japan, where it is readily available in **natto**, a fermented soybean dish that is very much an acquired taste if you live anywhere else. Interestingly, Japanese women who regularly eat natto have a lower incidence of bone fractures.[3,4] I will talk more about that in Chapters 2 and 4.

Unfortunately, in the Western world, Vitamin K—in all its forms—is difficult to get through the foods we eat. (More on that in Chapter 6.) Yes, you can get Vitamin K1 in broccoli, spinach, and kale. However, changes in agriculture and food manufacturing—such as fewer grass-fed animals and more processed foods—means that Vitamin K2 is not readily available in the food supply. Or it is available in inadequate amounts.

Fermented foods like mature cheeses and curd contain Vitamin K2, but those are harder to find and consistently consume in this world of packaged individual slices.

Outside of the Western world, natto, the traditional Japanese dish of fermented soybeans, is absolutely packed with all-natural Vitamin K2, but its taste has been described as "controversial." Even the smell is unpleasant to anyone outside of eastern Japan; most Westerners can't (or won't) stomach it.

For the time being, supplementation remains the best option.

Vitamin K's coagulation benefit has been known for almost 100 years. When were these benefits of Vitamin K2 discovered?

The promise of Vitamin K2 is a relatively recent development. In 1974, researchers discovered that promthobin, a factor in blood clotting, contained the Gla amino acid. Gla binds calcium ions and, more importantly, binds them to bone.[5,6] Research later determined that this could only happen with Vitamin K. As you might expect, scientists pursued new and interesting directions. Forty years later, we have a well-established body of research that clearly shows Vitamin K2—specifically Vitamin K2 as MK-7—as an important and effective member of the Vitamin K family with benefits that extend from childhood to our senior years.

And those benefits start with your heart and blood vessels.

Healthy Hints:

How Much Vitamin K2 is in Natto?

Simply put, a lot.

A 3.5-oz. serving of natto—less than a quarter of a pound—contains 1,103.4 micrograms of MK-7. That is a massive amount compared to egg yolks (15.5 micrograms) and whole milk (1.0 micrograms), both of which feature the less-effective form of Vitamin K2 as MK-4.[7]

 How does that amount affect your health? Studies in Japan showed a statistically significant inverse correlation in Japanese women who eat natto—which is usually served over rice and a raw egg—and the incidence of hip fractures.[3,4] The reason: high levels of Vitamin K2 as MK-7 activate more osteocalcin, the body's bone-building protein.[8,9] And, as we will discuss later, that process also helps to reduce calcification in the heart and the blood vessels.

The Japanese have been ingesting the natural Vitamin K2 found in natto for hundreds of years with no severe adverse effects. For every 100 grams of natto, there are 1,100 micrograms of MK-7[10,11], a massive amount compared to what is usually found in supplements. Statistics show that the annual consumption of natto per capita (90 million people) in Japan is 2 kilos. Some people eat much more; some much less.

Natto is an exotic dish that is mostly available in specialty stores. Even if you can find it, the dish is hard to swallow. Literally. So, unless you live in Japan or possess adventurous taste buds, it is best to obtain your Vitamin K2 from supplements.

DOCTOR'S IN(SIGHTS)

1) **Vitamins K1 and K2** belong to the **Vitamin K family**, but they differ in the length and degree of saturation of the carbon tail.

2) Studies have shown that **the most effective form of Vitamin K2 is MK-7**. With a longer half-life, it will be available to the body for a longer.

3) **The best way to get K2 is through supplementation.** The most abundant source, the Japanese dish natto, is basically inedible to Western palates. Modern diets, even healthy ones, do not provide nearly enough Vitamin K2 to help the body in a significant way.

4) The discovery of Vitamin K as a bone-building catalyst in 1974 paved the way for **exciting research involving Vitamin K2.**

NOTES

_____

_____

_____

_____

_____

_____

_____

_____

_____

_____

_____

_____

_____

_____

_____

_____

NOTES

Chapter 2

————◄O►————

How Does Vitamin K2 Protect My Heart?

"This year's birthday present from my wife was a heart scan, Dr. Goodman, even though I feel perfectly fine! I was shocked to learn that my result revealed early signs of blockages in my arteries to the heart! My physician told me I have cardiovascular disease and advised me to see a cardiologist. How did this happen and what do I need to do?"

Statistics—not predictions or worst-case scenarios—from the American Heart Association put the state of our heart health into grim perspective.[1] Here is a small overview:

- More than 787,000 people in the U.S. died from heart disease, stroke, or other cardiovascular diseases in 2010. That is about one of every three deaths in America.

- About 2,150 Americans die each day from these diseases, or one every 40 seconds.

- Cardiovascular diseases claim more lives than all forms of cancer combined.

- Direct and indirect costs of cardiovascular diseases and stroke total more than $315.4 billion. That includes health expenditures and lost productivity.

- From a worldwide perspective, heart disease is the No. 1 cause of death. It is also the leading cause of death in the United States, killing almost 380,000 Americans a year.

These frightening numbers only offer a glimpse into the deadliness of this silent killer. What do I mean by "silent killer"? By the time the symptoms of an unhealthy cardiovascular system manifest themselves, it could be too late to prevent serious events such as a heart attacks. That is why you have to have an action plan right now.

Just like this patient, seeing your physician is an important first step in determining your cardiovascular risk. There are many risk factors to consider, including smoking, high blood pressure, diabetes, family history, sleep apnea, obesity, physical inactivity, and stress. Paying attention to all of them could save your life.

I'm watching my cholesterol levels, both good and bad. Isn't that enough?

No. High cholesterol (better known as LDL) is only *one* of many risk factors. Typically, doctors urge patients to cut out fatty foods and sugar, lose weight, start exercising, and often prescribe medication like statins.

This is an appropriate strategy. However, as I wrote in my book *Magnificent Magnesium*, statins have been shown to reduce or prevent the recurrence of coronary events. The key word here is **recurrence**. A review of 11 large-scale studies covering some 65,000 patients, published in the *JAMA* (*Journal of the American Medical Association*) *Internal Medicine*, showed no evidence that statins had any benefits for heart disease prevention in patients who had not been previously diagnosed with a cardiovascular condition.[2] Even worse, you may have to endure some unpleasant side effects—such as muscle aches, headaches, and bloating—without any definite benefit.[3]

You must remember: cholesterol is one risk factor of *many* for heart disease. It is not the *cause* of heart disease.

In my own practice I discuss four keys to good health with every patient: nutrition (including supplements), exercise and flexibility, stress management, and sleep. These are the keys to wellness. Pharmaceuticals and nutraceuticals do not take care of everything. You have to do most of the work yourself. Ask any healthy person. They will readily admit how much time and energy they devote to maintaining good health.

What role does calcium play in cardiovascular health?

My patient's heart scan revealed that he had calcium deposits in his coronary arteries. Scientific studies have shown that the amount of calcium deposited in your arteries is an indicator of your underlying cardiovascular health. A heart scan can assess the amount of calcium in your coronary arteries—the higher the score, the greater your risk of a heart attack over the next five years.

A 2006 study in the journal *Atherosclerosis* looked at 10,000 asymptomatic people who were screened for five years for all-cause mortality. Researchers determined that survival rates were associated with the amount of calcium in the blood vessels. Using a linear prediction model, researchers determined that "a calcium score [less than] 10 resulted in a reduction in observed age by 10 years in subjects older than 70 years, while a calcium score [over] 400 added as much as *30 years of age* to younger patients."[4]

Calcium reflects what cardiologists call "hard plaque." Wherever you see hard plaque, there is the more dangerous "soft plaque" or "vulnerable plaque." This can rupture and cause an immediate blood clot, which leads to heart attack, stroke, and many of the aforementioned sobering statistics. Ironically, hard plaque can *protect us* from this rupture (i.e., it is part of the healing process), but it leads to narrowing of the blood vessels and reduced blood flow. Oxygen and vital nutrients do not get to the heart, which causes angina (chest pain due to lack of oxygen).

One might easily think it would be better to have healthy coronary arteries free of calcium and atherosclerosis, so why take calcium at all? Yes, we want our arteries free of calcium, but we cannot overlook the role calcium plays in our bodies, which I will address in Chapter 3.

We live in a society where people are focused on their looks and have no idea what's happening on the inside—of their arteries. Unfortunately, when we get the bad news, it is often too late. For 50 percent of the people who suffer a heart attack, it will be their first *and* last symptom of underlying heart disease.[5] I cannot stress this enough: look after your blood vessels! Keep them healthy, and you will extend your life by 10 years or more.

So what is Vitamin K2's role in the fight against calcification?

Vitamin K2 can play a major role in reducing blockages caused by atherosclerosis.

You have to dismiss the notion that calcification is inevitable as you age, or that it cannot be prevented. One important reason lies with the **matrix Gla protein (MGP).**

Calcium accumulation is strongly influenced by MGP. The proof came in a 1997 animal study in *Nature*, when researchers showed that mice without the ability to make MGP died after six to eight weeks. The reason: Massive calcification in the arteries.[6] Later studies confirmed that MGP is a key inhibitor of vascular calcification.[7-10]

For MGP to bind calcium—and thus keep it away from your blood vessels and arteries—it needs to be activated by Vitamin K2.

Here's how it works: K vitamin-dependent proteins such as MGP contain glutamic acid (Glu) residues. During **carboxylation**—when a carbon atom double-bonded to an oxygen atom and single-bonded to a hydroxyl group is introduced—Glu is transformed into gamma-carboxyglutamate (Gla) residues by the enzyme gamaglutamyl carboxylase.[11,12]

Gla binds calcium ions and ensures that calcium is deposited in the bones, where it needs to be. It keeps calcium away from the heart and the blood vessels, where it could cause damage. For all of this to happen, gamaglutamyl carboxylase needs Vitamin K2.

Vitamin K2 is known as a co-factor, but it is easier to think of Vitamin K2 as the finger that hits the light switch that causes the lights to turn on. The infrastructure to properly parcel out calcium in the body exists—just like the electrical wiring in your house—but it needs Vitamin K2 in the same way that a light switch needs that finger.

Here's the proof: In 2008, researchers measured the amount of undercarboxylated, or "inactive", MGP in the blood of healthy individuals and compared it to those with severe vascular diseases, including aortic stenosis (the narrowing of the heart's aortic valve). The study, published in *The Journal of Vascular Research*, showed that almost all the subjects with cardiovascular disease had undercarboxylated MGP levels below the normal adult range.[13]

So, to get back to the question you are probably asking, *"If calcium is so bad for my heart, why should I be taking a calcium supplement for my bones?"* I'll go into more detail in Chapter 3, but the short answer is yes. Calcium is essential for healthy, strong bones. Make sure you take it with Vitamin K2 so that calcium is deposited *and* kept in the bones where it is needed, and not in your heart and blood vessels, where it is a liability.

Which form of Vitamin K2 should I take?

Vitamin K2 in the form of MK-7 has a longer half-life, or stays in the body longer, than Vitamin K1 and other forms of K2. Vitamin K1 exits your body very quickly after it is utilized by the liver, and little is left for other tissues. Vitamin K2, on the other hand, is not excreted as quickly, which allows it to be recycled so the important Glu to Gla process can continue. One molecule of Vitamin K2 can carboxylate, or activate, about 500 molecules of proteins.

That is a good thing, since inactive MGP leads to calcification. A lack of Vitamin K2 results in undercarboxylation of MGP, which undermines the entire process. Research has shown an increased accumulation of undercarboxylated MGP in artheroscleroic plaques as well as other calcified areas.[13]

What does the research tell us?

Let's start with the evidence of Vitamin K2's role in calcification. An unpublished study examined biopsies of aortas from humans dying from cardiovascular diseases compared to aortic tissues from people who had died of other causes. It turned out that people with cardiovascular disease had lower amounts of Vitamin K1 and Vitamin K2 in the vessel wall. However, in healthy aortas, high levels of Vitamin K2 were found with barely detectable amounts of Vitamin K1, indicating Vitamin K2's vital role in keeping calcium out of the vessel wall.

Further evidence came from the landmark, large clinical study, the Rotterdam population cohort study, which looked at Vitamin K2 in a normal human population.

Results among 4,807 healthy individuals (at the start of the study) age 55 and older, suggested a strong protective effect of the highest dietary Vitamin K2 intake on arterial calcification. The study showed a reduction in risk for cardiovascular diseases and cardiovascular disease-related deaths by as much *as 50 percent* for subjects who ingested more Vitamin K2. High intakes of Vitamin K2 also reduced the all-cause mortality by *25 percent*.

Dietary vitamin K1, obtained from green vegetables, had no influence on excessive calcium accumulation, even when consumed in much larger quantities than K2.[14]

This was the first large clinical study to suggest the huge impact Vitamin K2 may play in reducing cardiovascular events and mortality. A positive, large, double-blind, randomized study would settle the issue. However, it is unlikely this trial will ever be done because of the huge expense involved. Still, what the Rotterdam Study revealed is quite promising.

Another study in *Nutrition, Metabolism, & Cardiovascular Diseases* looked at the effect of Vitamin K2 on arterial function, or the ability to contract and relax blood vessels. A group of 16,057 women (all free of cardiovascular diseases at baseline) aged 49-70 years were followed for eight years. The final results were again really promising: K2 vitamins were shown to reduce the risk of cardiovascular diseases. *The risk of coronary heart disease dropped nine percent* for every 10 micrograms of Vitamin K2 (MK-7, MK-8, and MK-9) subjects consumed. Vitamin K1 intake had no effect.[15]

Can I test for Vitamin K2 levels in my body?

Yes, you can, though not directly.

Right now, the most accurate measurement for Vitamin K levels is to determine the amount of the circulating undercarboxylated (inactive) form of the Vitamin K-dependent proteins in the blood, such as MGP.[16] The best option is an absolute ucOC test, which measures the amount of **osteocalcin**—another K-dependent protein—in the blood that is not activated by Vitamin K2.[17] Like MGP, Vitamin K2 is essential for carboxylating (activating) osteocalcin. Simply put, if your osteocalcin levels are undercarboxylated, that is an indicator of Vitamin K2 deficiency. (We will learn more about osteocalcin in the next chapter.)

Let's return to the heart and blood vessels, specifically how Vitamin K2 can improve arterial function.

One way to measure healthy arterial function—the ability of a vessel to contract and relax—is through pulse wave velocity. Arterial dysfunction, better known as endothelial dysfunction, is one of the early signs of atherosclerosis. It is often present long before blockages occur.

A particularly exciting study recently published online in *Thrombosis and Haemostasis* shows Vitamin K2's positive effect on arterial function using doppler pulse wave velocity.[18]

In a three-year, double-blind study, 244 healthy post-menopausal Dutch women were randomly assigned to receive daily either 180 micrograms of Vitamin K2 as MK-7 or placebo capsules. Using pulse wave velocity and ultrasound techniques, the trial showed significant improvement in arterial stiffness (that is to say improved arterial elasticity) especially in women who had stiff arteries at baseline.

This is the first human study using Vitamin K2 to show improvement in arterial function and prove significant benefit of K2 on cardiovascular health.

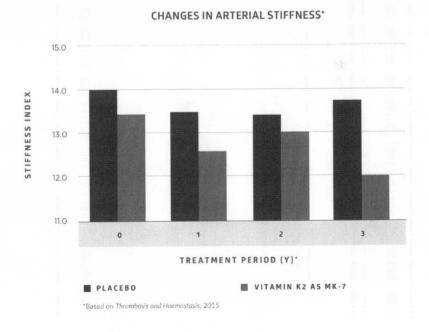

CHANGES IN ARTERIAL STIFFNESS*

*Based on *Thrombosis and Haemostasis*, 2015

Healthy Hints:

What Else Should I Do For My Heart?

Vitamin K2 is only one factor in reducing your cardiovascular risk. Achieving optimal cardiovascular health requires lifestyle changes, as well as supplementation. Here are my recommendations:

- **Adjust your diet and fitness goals—slowly and steadily.** Legumes, vegetables, and fruits are high in fiber. Fish, especially salmon, are ripe with heart-healthy omega-3 fatty acids. Both are terrific for your heart. Make the changes gradually so you are not overwhelmed and frustrated when or if you cannot stick to your new food pyramid.

- **Regarding fitness, you do not need to run a marathon or live at the gym.** To start, try a brisk walk or a bike ride, and do it with a friend so you can stay motivated. All you need is 20 to 30 minutes. You can even incorporate exercise into your daily life: take the stairs instead of the elevator. Walk to the bank to deposit a check instead of using your phone. Garden. Mow the lawn.

- **Steps #1 and #2 are crucial to follow if you are overweight.** Lugging around extra pounds strains your heart, and can contribute to other factors for heart disease such as diabetes, high blood cholesterol, and cholesterol. There is a strong likelihood you are in this camp: According to the Centers for Disease Control and Prevention (CDC), almost 70 percent of American adults over the age of 20 are either overweight or obese.[20,21]

- **Find time to reduce stress.** Meet up with a friend, squeeze a rubber ball, or even try yoga or meditation—you can do that just about anywhere. Yes, work and family matters stretch us to the limit, but find 30 minutes a day that is just for you. Think of this as a required recharging, not slacking off on the job.

- **Take your vitamins.** Not just vitamin K2. There are a variety of supplements you can take to help bridge the nutritional gap, such as vitamin D, magnesium, fish oil in form of krill oil (a superior source of omega-3s), and more. Talk to your doctor about your best options for supplementation, diet, and exercise. He or she knows you best and can give you sound advice. If you do not have a regular physician, find one who has an open mind to supplements and a holistic approach to health.

You can also test for atherosclerosis, before any symptoms occur, by undergoing a calcium scan or a heart scan, which determines the volume and density of calcium in your coronary arteries. The number represents your arterial calcium burden, and reflects the buildup of plaque. As we discussed previously, undercarboxylated MGP reflects low Vitamin K2 levels and correlates with the severity of arterial calcification. The greater the degree of Vitamin K2 deficiency, the more likely you are to have calcium in the coronary arteries, and a higher scan score.

I'm taking an anti-coagulant right now. Is it safe for me to take Vitamin K2?

Studies have shown that a low dose (45 micrograms) of Vitamin K2 as MK-7 is unlikely to interfere with blood-thinning medications and does not provoke any risk of clot formation inside the blood vessels.[12]

However, if you are on any blood thinning medications, you should first consult your doctor before taking Vitamin K2.

How safe is Vitamin K2?

It is regarded as extremely safe. There is no documented case of known toxicity for Vitamin K1 and Vitamin K2. The European Food Safety Authority (EFSA) determined that menaquinones as a source of Vitamin K were safe in low doses, although it offers no specific number. According to the EFSA in 2008, "natto-derived MK-7 has been authorized for use in foods for particular nutritional uses, food supplements, and foods intended for the general population in the European Union."[19]

In all of the research studies using Vitamin K2, there have been no reports of severe adverse effects, including reproductive studies.

R℞ DOCTOR'S IN(SIGHTS)

1) Cardiovascular disease is the **No. 1 killer in the Western World**, so it is important to have a game plan for your cardiovascular health right now.

2) **The matrix GLA protein (MGP)** binds calcium and ensures that it stays in the bones and away from the heart. MGP requires Vitamin K2 to be fully functional via a process called **carboxylation.**

3) Studies have shown the **superiority of Vitamin K2** over Vitamin K1 in reducing the risk of calcification.

4) There have been **no known adverse or toxic events related** to oral K2 supplementation or through the consumption of natto, the most abundant source of Vitamin K2 as MK-7. But before you take Vitamin K2, check with your doctor, especially if you are taking anticoagulants.

5) Optimizing your cardiovascular health requires making gradual, **steady changes to your diet, exercise habits, and stress levels**.

NOTES

_____

_____

_____

_____

_____

_____

_____

_____

_____

_____

_____

_____

_____

_____

_____

NOTES

Chapter 3

———◆⟨O⟩◆———

Why Is Vitamin K2 Good For Bone Health?

"Dr. Goodman, I just had a bone scan. It turns out that I have osteopenia, which I understand can lead to osteoporosis. My physician started me on calcium supplements, but I just read it is advisable to take calcium with Vitamin K2. Do you agree?"

Like the heart and the blood vessels, the health of our bones is something we usually do not think about much. Then, a problem arises—such as a hip fracture—and just like the cardiovascular system, it is too late to make any real impact.

Bone health is important throughout your life. Osteoporosis and bone fractures are not just the problems of old age. As with cardiovascular health, your skeleton matters more than superficial appearance.

Why should I be concerned about my bones?

The numbers tell an alarming story about bone health, specifically the impact of **osteoporosis**, which is when bone loss exceeds bone growth:

- Worldwide, osteoporosis causes more than 8.9 million fractures annually, resulting in an osteoporotic fracture every three seconds.[1]

- As of 1997, osteoporosis affected 75 million people in the U.S., Japan, and Europe.[2]

- Worldwide, osteoporosis affects 200 million women, according to a 2007 report.[3]

With osteoporosis, the bones are more likely to fracture, which could lead to a diminished quality of life—or worse.

"Of particular concern are vertebral (spinal) and hip fractures," according to the International Osteoporosis Foundation. "Vertebral fractures can result in serious consequences, including loss of height, intense back pain, and [spinal] deformity (sometimes called Dowager's Hump)." Hip fractures typically require surgery, leading to more problems. Patients frequently develop hospital-related pneumonia, which can be fatal. When a patient leaves the hospital, walkers, canes, and other aids could chip away at their independence.

Prescription drugs are often used, but they are fraught with unpleasant side effects. The most popular class of prescription drugs for osteoporosis, bisphosphanates, has been shown in some people to *increase* the loss of bone in the jaw as well as contributing to gastrointestinal stress and bone pain.[4]

How do the bones get to this point?

The entire skeleton is replaced every seven to 10 years through an active process called **remodeling**. This process involves **osteoblasts** (cells that build up the skeleton) and **osteoclasts** (cells that break down the skeleton).

Now, as long as the bone-building activity of osteoblasts (**absorption**) exceeds the bone-destructive action of osteoclasts (**resorption**), the process of maintaining bones remains healthy. If the ratio is reversed, bone density is significantly reduced (bone tissue erodes slowly and steadily) along with the quality of bone. The bones lose strength. This is the result of osteoporosis, which eventually leads to those dreaded fractures.

Again, most of us do not realize our bones are in this kind of shape until the worst comes. Women are generally more prone to osteoporosis because they have less bone mass than men, and their annual loss of bone mass is accelerated after menopause.

The risk of osteoporosis affects everyone. Consider that we typically reach peak bone mass by our early 30s. Once we reach that peak, that is the most bone mass we will ever have, and it simply declines from there. The best we can do is maintain our bones to slow that decline, meaning that our bones must be nourished and kept in top condition so they can last our whole lives.

What is Vitamin K2's role in the bones?

- Osteoblasts, our bone builders, produce a protein called **osteocalcin.**

- Osteocalcin must first be activated (or carboxylated) by Vitamin K2 to properly bind calcium to bones.

- Calcium is essential to maintain bone strength and to inhibit osteoporosis and fracture.

Once again, Vitamin K2 is the "finger" that hits the light switch. Without Vitamin K2, you can't "turn on" (activate) osteocalcin, which takes calcium where it is needed—and keeps it there.

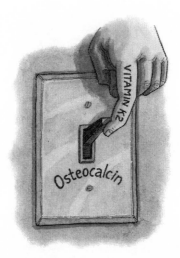

Research in the 1980s found that patients with hip fractures had low levels of Vitamin K in their blood.[5] This was one of the first clues that Vitamin K is essential for healthy bones.

Several studies since then have confirmed low levels of Vitamin K2 in patients with osteoporotic fractures.[6-13] Vitamin K2 as MK-7 is the most effective form of Vitamin K because it is more readily absorbed and has a longer half-life. In other words, MK-7 lasts longer in the body.

The richest source of Vitamin K2 as MK-7 is natto, the fermented soybean dish that I discussed in Chapter 1. A 2001 study in *Nutrition*, showed that people with high natto intake had a reduced risk of fracture.[14] In 2006, a clinical study featuring 944 women, ranging in age from 20 to 79, linked natto consumption to inhibiting loss of bone mineral density.[15]

However, longer study periods are required to effectively measure the positive effects on bones. For example, a 2013 Dutch randomized study in *Osteoporosis International* featured 244 healthy post-menopausal women, who were given either placebo capsules or 180 micrograms of MK-7 over a

Healthy Hints:

What Can I Do To Prevent Osteoporosis?

You can do many things actually: maintain a proper weight, exercise, and take supplements (including calcium, magnesium, zinc, and Vitamin K2.) In fact, all are necessary to achieve optimal bone health. Vitamin K2 is simply a small part in the gradual renovation of your lifestyle, one that starts with awareness and continues with healthier choices.

As I discussed in my book, *Magnificent Magnesium*, diet has much to do with our rickety bones. Medical anthropologist Susan Brown has observed that cultures that grow their own food have significantly less osteoporosis than Americans and Europeans. Unfortunately, the diet in the Western world features acidifying food and beverages that contain refined carbohydrates, excessive animal protein, and sugar. These elements contribute to osteoporosis and heart disease.

Traditional diets are replete with non-acidic foods: broccoli, bananas, spinach, etc. These foods help maintain a healthy balance in the body. The development and accumulation of acids sets the stage for disease. A diet featuring fresh foods is a great asset in maintaining a proper pH balance. So is supplementation with minerals such as Vitamin K2, magnesium, and vitamin D. Calcium is crucial—if taken correctly.

Exercise is also essential for preventing bone loss and maintaining muscle strength. The International Osteoporosis Foundation recommends 30 to 40 minutes three to four times each week, with some weight-bearing and resistance exercises thrown in. Of course, you should talk to your doctor before starting an exercise program.

You already know that women, especially post-menopausal women, and organ transplant recipients are at greater risk of developing osteoporosis. Other risk factors for osteoporosis include obesity, age, family history, trauma, and muscle weakness.

three-year span. The women who took MK-7 had less circulating inactive (undercarboxylated) osteocalcin, indicating higher Vitamin K2 levels in the body. Via a bone mineral density test (DXA), researchers saw better bone mineral density and bone strength in these women.[16]

Vitamin K2 can be considered an important nutrient for bone health along with well-known nutrients such as calcium, magnesium, zinc, and vitamin D, where **Vitamin K2 serves as a complement.** A 2012 study in *Calcified Tissue International* examined the effect of dairy products enriched with calcium, vitamin D(3), and Vitamin K1 or K2 (as MK-7) on bone metabolism in postmenopausal women after 12 months. Researchers observed significant increases in bone mineral density and showed "more favorable changes" in bone metabolism and bone mass versus the control group.[17]

A 2008 study in the *Journal of Epidemiology* highlighted Vitamin K2, again from natto, as a key component for improved bone health. Vitamin K2 consumption was strongly associated with lowering the risk of hip fractures, indicating an important role of MK-7 in the prevention of disability and mortality. Many elderly people die in the hospital, often from infections (such as pneumonia) or blood clots that travel from the legs to the lungs as a complication of hip or leg fractures.[18] In fact, 25 percent of elderly patients who suffer a hip or leg fracture die within one year.

Another group facing an increased risk of osteoporosis is organ transplant recipients. One possible explanation is the treatment of the disease. For example, sometimes the medication—given pre- or post-transplant—can lead to osteoporosis. A 2010 Norwegian study involving 35 lung and 59 heart transplant recipients showed that the group treated with Vitamin K2 (180 micrograms of MK-7) had higher bone mineral density and bone mineral content in the lumbar spine. These results occurred even though many of the participants were deficient in vitamin D.[19]

Is there a way I can determine my Vitamin K2 levels as they relate to my bone health?

Testing is in the early stages, so few tests are readily available for the public. The best option, for now, is to take an **absolute ucOC test.** This measures the amount of osteocalcin in the blood not activated by Vitamin K2. Undercarboxylated osteocalcin (ucOC) is an indicator of Vitamin K2 status. The more inactive osteocalcin you have, the lower the range of Vitamin K2.[20]

It is more difficult for a doctor to discern Vitamin K status in the blood because the very little K one consumes is actually stored in the body. So, looking at levels of a K-dependent protein, such as osteocalcin, is a more accurate reflection of Vitamin K2 status.

I also recommend getting a bone density scan to evaluate your fracture risk. Men and women should get one at age 65 regardless of their health.[21] However, your risk for osteoporosis doubles if you are a woman over 65, or a man or woman over 50 with any of the following risk factors:

- Personal history of fracture as an adult[20]
- Low body weight or thin body stature
- Cigarette smoking
- Use of corticosteroid therapy for more than three months
- Impaired vision
- Estrogen deficiency at an early age
- Dementia
- Poor health/frailty
- Frequent falls
- Low calcium intake
- Low physical activity
- Having more than two alcoholic drinks per day
- Suffering from thyroid disease or rheumatoid arthritis
- Excessive caffeine consumption (e.g., caffeine, soda)
- Use of oral conception

Is there any relationship between osteoporosis and cardiovascular disease?

Many similarities exist. Both diseases can develop over decades before visible—and possibly fatal—symptoms occur. It affects both men and women, and the resulting cost in medical care can be crippling to patients and their families.

A Norwegian study from 2004 including 2,543 men and 2,726 postmenopausal women (55-74 years old) demonstrated that women with low bone density scores had a higher incidence of *calcified atherosclerotic plaques*.[22] Another study followed a group of healthy post-menopausal women for eight years. During that time, a strong association between the progression of aortic calcification (which increased every year) and bone loss emerged. Women with the highest gain in calcification had four times greater yearly bone loss than similarly aged women with low calcification.[23]

A 1993 study in *The Journal of Clinical Investigation*, found calcification of the artery wall due to atherosclerosis-contained elements from bone tissue.[24] Extensive research further established a connection. A meta-analysis of 70 human studies representing nearly 32,000 subjects—published in *Arthritis Research and Therapy* in 2011—concluded that patients with subclinical cardiovascular disease (i.e., not symptomatic) had six times the risk of developing bone loss and fractures. Patients with lower bone mass had a higher incidence of cardiovascular events (such as stroke) and death.[25]

DOCTOR'S IN(SIGHTS)

1) Like cardiovascular health, **problems involving your bones build over decades**. The earlier you address this, the better you will be throughout your life.

2) **Osteoporosis** occurs when bone loss exceeds bone growth, which leads to fractures and other painful conditions.

3) Bone-building **osteoblasts** produce a protein called **osteocalcin**, which binds calcium to bone. But osteocalcin must first be activated by Vitamin K2.

4) Certain groups have a higher risk for osteoporosis, including women, smokers, and the obese, but **we are all at risk.**

5) **Exercise** and a **healthy diet are also vital to the health of your bones**. Taking calcium, vitamin D, Vitamin K2, and magnesium are important to reduce this risk of osteoporosis and to improve cardiovascular health.

NOTES

NOTES

_____

_____

_____

_____

_____

_____

_____

_____

_____

_____

_____

_____

_____

_____

Chapter 4

——◄◦►——

Why Can't I Just Take Calcium?

"Dr. Goodman, I've been eating a lot of dairy since I was kid. Now, in my mid-40s, I put skim milk in my smoothie, Swiss cheese on my turkey sandwich, and feta in my salad. Do I still a need calcium supplement?"

As soon as we entered the world, we encountered calcium. We got it in our bottles and in those small milk cartons during snack time in school. At dinner, our parents would urge us to drink a tall glass of milk so we would grow big and strong. Then, the food industry started taking care of this for us by fortifying our breakfast cereals, orange juice, and a slew of other items found in the supermarket with calcium.

Calcium is an essential mineral, but it has a potential downside.

Here are the positives: Calcium provides structure and hardness to bones and teeth; allows muscles to contract and nerves to send signals; makes blood vessels constrict and relax; helps the heart to pump; and supports protein function and hormone regulation.[1] Calcium supplementation is supported by several studies backing its benefits for bone health and osteoporosis prevention, as well as for overall health.

So what's the catch with calcium?

Several studies have shown that calcium may also do harm. You very well may be strengthening your bones at the expense of your heart and blood vessels.

In 2013, a *JAMA Internal Medicine* study examined the National Institutes of Health (NIH)–AARP Diet and Health Study, which evaluated the role of supplemental calcium on cardiovascular health.[2] The background: nearly 200,000 men and 169,000 women had their health status followed over 12 years. The researchers found that men—but not women—taking more than 1,000 milligrams a day of calcium supplements had a *20 percent higher risk* of cardiovascular death compared to those taking no calcium supplements.

Initially, this looked like women were in the clear. However, data from the Women's Health Initiative showed that those taking 1,000 milligrams of calcium supplements a day increased their risk of cardiovascular events by 15 to 22 percent.[3] This especially applied to women who did not take calcium at the beginning of the study. These findings were also independent of vitamin D. In other words, the risk remained the same whether an additional 400 IU a day of vitamin D was part of someone's diet.

In another study looking at the role of calcium with vitamin D supplementation, researchers found a 24 percent increased risk of coronary heart disease among 10,555 Finish women who used calcium supplements. Again, the risk was the same regardless of vitamin D intake.[4]

Also, researchers from the European Prospective Investigation into Cancer and Nutrition study (EPIC-Heidelberg) concluded that in the 23,980 participants, those regularly taking a calcium supplement had an *86 percent higher* risk for heart attack compared to those who did not. In subjects who supplemented with calcium alone, the risk of heart attack more than doubled.[5]

Further, diseased populations could also anticipate problems supplementing with calcium, specifically those suffering from chronic kidney disease and mineral bone disorder (CKD-MBD).

CKD-MBD occurs when the kidneys fail to maintain the proper levels of calcium and phosphorus in the blood, leading to abnormal bone hormone levels—and an increased risk for osteoporosis.[6]

Kidney patients are also at an increased risk of heart disease due to calcium being deposited in the arteries.

Healthy Hints:

What Else Do I Need To Know About Calcium?

- The average daily recommended intake of calcium differs with age. Males and females—from age 4 to 70+—need anywhere from 1,000 to 1,300 milligrams a day. In reality, we need more. Children, teens, and the aging population need the most.[14]

- Even though dairy products represent a rich source of calcium, approximately 43 percent of the U.S. population and 70 percent of older women regularly take calcium supplements.[15]

- Calcium is the most abundant nutrient in humans. Bones and teeth store 99 percent of the body's calcium; it provides hardness and structure.[16]

- Muscles, nerves, and blood vessels depend on the remaining one percent of calcium for their function.[16]

Patients with CKD-MBD should not take calcium supplements. In patients with kidney failure, supplemental calcium has also been linked to increased atherosclerosis, as well as higher mortality.[7,8] Published in *The Lancet,* this 2013 meta-analysis—that is combining and analyzing the results from different studies—of kidney disease found that calcium supplementation was associated with a 22 percent increased risk of cardiovascular death in more than 4,600 patients.[9]

The message is clear: Calcium supplementation, with or without vitamin D, results in increased cardiovascular risk. The mechanism is most likely calcium deposition in blood vessels resulting in abnormal arterial function (i.e., endothelial dysfunction) and blockages in the arteries.

If I am at an increased risk for cardiovascular disease, should I be taking calcium at all?

The answer, in my opinion, is definitely YES. Calcium is essential for healthy bones and all the benefits mentioned earlier. The question is: how can we avoid the cardiovascular risk?

When you take calcium, it us supposed to head to the bone. That is good. However, calcium can also get deposited in the blood vessels, where it contributes to calcification and possible blockages. That is bad. This is called the **calcium paradox**.[10]

Vitamin K2 is the solution to the calcium paradox.

It is not enough to consume dietary calcium. It needs to be managed and properly utilized. Vitamin K2 activates the **matrix Gla protein (MGP)** and **osteocalcin**, the two proteins responsible for inhibiting calcium mineralization in the arteries, and for binding calcium to the bone matrix, respectively. Put simply, the activation of these proteins ensures calcium goes to the bone and not the blood vessels.

When taking a calcium supplement, it is advisable to also take Vitamin K2, specifically as MK-7. If you do not, you risk losing the benefit of calcium to your bones and increasing the risk to your heart. Supplements containing combinations of calcium, vitamin D, and Vitamin K2 are available in health food stores, drug stores, and at reputable online vendors. I would recommend one of those over just a calcium supplement.

What is the evidence to support this recommendation?

The Rotterdam Study[11] showed that a relatively high dietary intake of Vitamin K2 has a strong protective effect on heart health. In this 2004 study published in *The Journal of Nutrition*, over 4,800 men and women above age 55 at the start of the study were followed for 10 years. Dietary intake of vitamin K was closely monitored. The risk of coronary heart disease incidents, all-cause mortality, and aortic atherosclerosis were studied in tertiles (i.e., groups) of energy-adjusted vitamin K intake after adjustment for age, gender, BMI, smoking, diabetes, education, and dietary factors.

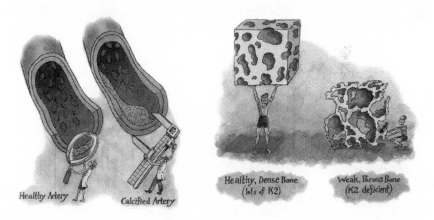

Healthy Artery   Calcified Artery   Healthy, Dense Bone (lots of K2)   Weak, Porous Bone (K2 deficient)

The results showed that subjects consuming the highest amount of natural vitamin K2 in their diet (an average of 45 micrograms of K2 per day) reduced the risk of both arterial calcification and cardiovascular death by as much as *50 percent*—with no undesirable side effects.

An important point to remember is that longer trial periods are required to track any changes in heart and bone health, and whether Vitamin K2 supplementation in fact makes a difference. (This is not like weight loss where one can tell in weeks whether they have dropped a pant size.) Thankfully, researchers committed to such study have been able to provide another step guiding us in the right direction.

A clinical trial for Vitamin K2 as MK-7 supplementation provided a statistically significant protection of vulnerable bone structures.[12] Bone mineral density of lumbar spine, total hip, and femoral neck were measured by DXA; bone strength indices of the femoral neck were calculated. Vertebral fracture assessment was performed by DXA and used as a measure for vertebral fractures. The ucOC/cOC ratio served as marker of vitamin K status. Measurements occurred at baseline and after one, two, and three years of treatment.

A key finding from this study, which was published in *Osteoporosis International,* is that clinically relevant improvement at the site of the femoral neck became evident after two to three years of 180 micrograms a day of MK-7 supplementation. Also, researchers observed a *decrease* in the age-related decline in bone mineral content and bone mineral density at the lumbar spine.

Importantly, heart health measurements were also taken of this study's participants over three years, the results of which have been published online in *Thrombosis and Haemostasis.*[13] This trial also showed substantial benefits in inhibiting age-related stiffening of arteries in the placebo group, but not in the MK-7 group. Supplementation also resulted in a *statistically significant improvement* of vascular elasticity. This is the first human study using Vitamin K2 to confirm an actual *improvement* in arterial function.

DOCTOR'S IN(SIGHTS)

1) **Calcium is essential** for strong, healthy bones and other bodily functions, but taken alone it may be harmful.

2) The **calcium paradox** is that, as much as we need calcium, particularly for strong bones, it can potentially harm the cardiovascular system.

3) **Vitamin K2, especially as MK-7, is the answer to that calcium paradox** because it binds calcium to the bone matrix (where it belongs) and keeps it away from the heart and blood vessels (where it does not).

4) If you supplement with calcium, it is advisable that you also **take Vitamin K2 to ensure proper calcium utilization**.

NOTES

NOTES

Chapter 5

—◄O►—

When Should I Consider Taking Vitamin K2?

"Dr. Goodman, I take Vitamin K2 daily, and I think it might be a good addition to my child's supplement routine. What do you think?

At this point, you have realized that prevention is one of this book's main themes. Vitamin K2 is an integral part of your healthy self-awareness, one that involves the right diet, consistent exercise, and good lifestyle choices.

The secret is that this attitude adjustment does not have to start in our 30s or 40s, when most of us begin thinking about our own mortality. Healthy lives should start in childhood. This is where parents are so influential in their actions, whether it is packing a healthy lunch for their children or making exercise part of family time.

Those small steps can have a huge impact. Why? The conditions that plague us as adults—specifically the cardiovascular and bone issues I have detailed—are rooted in childhood. These problems do not appear out of thin air; they take years to develop. Maintaining good health will enhance our golden years, that time when we get to do some of the things we have always wanted to do.

This chapter will explain why childhood is such an important time in our health history, and the role Vitamin K2 plays in ensuring a child's healthy adulthood.

At what age are children typically exposed to Vitamin K?

Vitamin K supplementation is important from an early age. Keep in mind that your child has been consuming Vitamin K from the moment he or she was born. Aside from Vitamin K being given to newborns immediately after birth to help with normal blood coagulation, it is present in a mother's breast milk (provided she has adequate Vitamin K intake)[1], and formula milk is fortified with higher vitamin K levels than breast milk.[2]

However, Vitamin K deficiency, even without bleeding, may occur in as many as 50 percent of infants younger than 5 days old.[3] Unfortunately, breastfeeding is not the best source of Vitamin K. Infants who are exclusively breastfed during their first six months of life get less than 1 microgram a day. That is 100 times *lower* than what infants are fed in a supplemented formula.[4]

Why should my child take Vitamin K2?

The first and best course of action is to talk to your child's pediatrician about whether he or she should start taking Vitamin K2. But I can certainly provide some reasons why it should be considered.

We have already discussed how Vitamin K2 activates osteocalcin, the protein that helps attach calcium to the bone matrix and is a crucial component of the bone-building process.

Childhood is, without question, the most important time for the growth of bones. Bone tissue grows and develops most intensely during childhood and adolescence. Consequently, it is when the need for active osteocalcin and K vitamins is *greatest*.

The reason? *Ninety percent* of your peak bone mass is attained by age 18 for girls and 20 for boys. By our early 30s, you reach peak bone mass, and once you reach that peak, it is the most you will ever have. The higher the bone mass acquired before ages 20 to 25, the better the prognosis for bone health later in life. (Just a *10 percent increase* in bone mass is estimated to reduce the risk of osteoporotic fracture in adult life by 50 percent.)[5]

So the better your Vitamin K status as a child—especially in puberty—the better chance you have to prevent bone-related disorders later in life.

How Vitamin K2 deficient are children?

The deficiency in Vitamin K persists after infancy. Poor diets and changes in how our food is raised and produced have increased the need for supplemental Vitamin K2. A 2014 study published in *Food & Function* revealed that healthy children have the largest tissue-specific Vitamin K deficiency, followed by adults 40 years and older. Not only should your child take Vitamin K2, they *need* to take it.[6]

A 2005 British study in *Public Health Nutrition* compared dietary intake and sources of Vitamin K in 4,599 4-year-old children born in the 1950s and 307 children in the 1990s. Results showed that dietary Vitamin K intake was significantly higher (P<0.001) in the 1950s (39 micrograms a day) compared with the 1990s (24 micrograms a day).[7]

The decrease in children's Vitamin K intake could help explain an unfortunate result of rough-and-tumble childhoods.

Forearm fractures are a common occurrence for children around puberty, possibly because children's physical activity increases at the same time that there is less cortical bone mass due to the increased calcium demand during skeletal growth. A 2003 population-based research study[8] in Minnesota examined forearm fractures in children during four time periods spanning 1969 to 2001.

The annual incidence rates of forearm fractures per 100,000

increased significantly from 263.3 in 1969-1971 to 322.3 in 1979-1981, and to 399.8 in 1989-1991 before leveling off at 372.9 in 1999-2001. Age-adjusted incidence rates per 100,000 were 32 percent greater among males in 1999-2001 compared with 1969-1971 (P =0.01), and 56 percent greater among females in the same time periods (P<0.001).

Another study conducted in Denmark showed similar findings: The fracture rate increased by 33 percent in girls and 5 percent in boys between 1975 to 1979 and 1985.[9]

As we have discussed, **undercarboxylated (inactive) osteocalcin** levels reflect a low Vitamin K2 status. Research has shown that children have *eight to 10 times* more undercarboxylated osteocalcin.

A study of the Vitamin K status in the bones of 86 healthy children and 30 adults confirmed this. A marked elevation of the ratio of undercarboxylated osteocalcin (uOC) to carboxylated (activated) osteocalcin (cOC) was observed in the children. Additionally, a marked correlation between the bone markers for bone metabolism and ucOC and cOC was found in the children's group.[10]

These studies suggest children are Vitamin K2 deficient at a crucial in bone development.

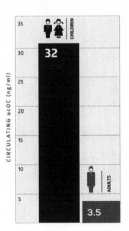

INACTIVE K STATUS IN HEALTHY VOLUNTEERS

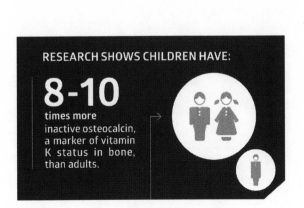

RESEARCH SHOWS CHILDREN HAVE:

8-10 times more inactive osteocalcin, a marker of vitamin K status in bone, than adults.

How has Vitamin K2 been shown to help kids?

This is an exciting, emerging field of research.

Researchers in Europe investigated the relationship between the serum percentage of **undercarboxylated osteocalcin**, bone mineral density, and biochemical markers of bone turnover in 223 11- and 12-year-old healthy girls. (These are the ages when dynamic bone development occurs.) Results, published in *The British Journal of Nutrition* in 2007, demonstrated that better Vitamin K status was associated with increased bone mineral density of the total body ($P < 0.001$) and lumbar spine ($P < 0.05$) in healthy girls.[11]

Another study featuring 245 healthy girls ranging from 3 to 16 years of age examined whether vitamin intake and markers of Vitamin K status were related to bone mineral content, as well as bone resorption (break down) over four years. Better Vitamin K status (high plasma Vitamin K and low undercarboxylated osteocalcin) was associated with lower bone resorption. In short, better Vitamin K status—*at least 45 micrograms a day*—was associated with better bone health in healthy girls consuming a typical U.S. diet. The results were published in *The American Journal of Clinical Nutrition* in 2004.[12]

Further, researchers also conducted an eight-week, double-blind, randomized, placebo-controlled trial in which 45 micrograms of Vitamin K2 as MK-7 was given to healthy prepubescent children. The placebo group displayed no significant changes in ucOC, cOC, the ratio of ucOC to cOC, and MK-7, while kids who took the Vitamin K2 supplement saw increased osteocalcin carboxylation. The 2009 *British Journal of Nutrition* study concluded, in other words, that more calcium found its way to the bones.[13]

The effects of Vitamin K2 as MK-7 have also been examined in children with certain blood disorders. In a 2013 *Journal of Pediatric Hematology/Oncology* study, 20 children with thalassemic osteopathy (TOSP)—a blood disorder that may result in osteopenia and osteoporosis—were given a dietary supplement with Vitamin K2 (50 micrograms Vitamin K2 as MK-7) and vitamin D (5 micrograms calcitriol).[14]

Results from the prospective, one-year pilot study showed a significant improvement in the bone mineral density at the lumbar spine area of the patients at six months and 12 months of the treatment, especially in prepubescent girls. Vitamin K2 and calcitriol combination positively affected the TOSP-affected BMD of the children.

Are there any known risks of children taking Vitamin K2?

No severe adverse effects of natto (the primary food source of Vitamin K2) or Vitamin K2 as MK-7 have been reported. There have been no adverse or toxic effects linked to acute or long-term oral animal treatment of Vitamin K2 in the form of MK-4 or MK-7, nor have there been any toxic effects reported in reproductive studies.[15-19] Vitamin K2 as MK-7 is *the most effective form of Vitamin K.*

Healthy Hints:

What Are The Recommended Intake Levels For Vitamin K2?

There are currently no agreed upon recommended daily intakes for Vitamin K2. The numbers represented in the chart are for Vitamin K in general, not for Vitamin K2.

While benefits have been demonstrated in studies where children supplemented K2 as MK-7 at the 45-50 mcg/day level, the inteneed to improve K2 status in children warrants further discussion to establish whether this dose is in fact adequate in comparison to what growing children actually need.[20]

The Adequate Intake levels of vitamin K* for children, as established by the Food and Nutrition Board, Institute of Medicine:			
LIFE STAGE	**AGE**	**FEMALES/ MALES** mcg/day	**K2**
INFANTS	0-6 months	2.0	?
INFANTS	7-12 months	2.5	?
CHILDREN	1-3 years	30	?
CHILDREN	4-8 years	55	?
CHILDREN	9-13 years	60	?

* DOSES ESTABLISHED FOR K1 BASED ON EFFECTS ON COAGULATION SYSTEM

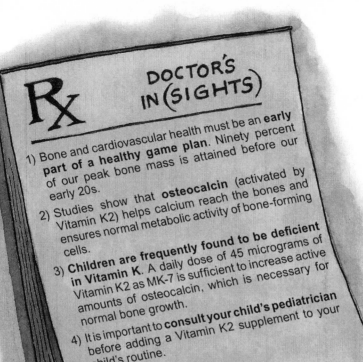

R_X DOCTOR'S IN(SIGHTS)

1) Bone and cardiovascular health must be an **early part of a healthy game plan**. Ninety percent of our peak bone mass is attained before our early 20s.

2) Studies show that **osteocalcin** (activated by Vitamin K2) helps calcium reach the bones and ensures normal metabolic activity of bone-forming cells.

3) **Children are frequently found to be deficient in Vitamin K**. A daily dose of 45 micrograms of Vitamin K2 as MK-7 is sufficient to increase active amounts of osteocalcin, which is necessary for normal bone growth.

4) It is important to **consult your child's pediatrician** before adding a Vitamin K2 supplement to your child's routine.

NOTES

NOTES

_____

_____

_____

_____

_____

_____

_____

_____

_____

_____

_____

_____

_____

_____

_____

_____

_____

Chapter 6

◄○►

Where Can I Get Vitamin K2?

"Dr. Goodman, I'm eating really well. The only sweets I touch are fruits. Beer and mixed drinks are gone. I have cut out fast food. I eat fish a few times a week and stick to organic lean meats. I eat a green vegetable at least once a day. Do I still need to take Vitamin K2?"

Like my patient, many of you probably think that a healthy diet will give you all the nutrients you need. I am afraid it does not always work that way. I always favor using natural plant-based resources for obtaining adequate amounts of vitamins and minerals. However, because our current diet has many gaps, certain nutrients are extremely difficult to achieve from diet alone.

The richest dietary source of Vitamin K2 as MK-7 is natto, which is eaten in certain parts of Japan—and avoided (by choice) everywhere else. The Japanese can get Vitamin K2 without supplementation, but not here in the states or in most places around the world, the best Western source of Vitamin K2 is hard-rind cheeses like gouda and goose liver pate, which are not exactly lunch box staples.

Adequate Vitamin K2 is virtually non-existent in today's food supply, and this is especially true for Vitamin K2's best form, MK-7. Unfortunately, the food industry has not fortified many foods—such as breakfast cereals—with Vitamin K2 the way it has with folic acid and calcium.

For now, supplementation remains your best option.

Why is Vitamin K2 not abundant in the food supply?

Remember, we get many of our nutrients from food sources. We get what they eat. How animals are raised and produce is grown is not what it once was.

The first cattle feedlots opened in 1950; poultry moved from pasture to buildings later in the decade. Dairy farmers and pork producers made the move in the 1960s and 1970s, respectively. That transition from grass-fed to commercial feed—which featured less Vitamin K1—was a real blow for Vitamin K2 in the diet. Grass-grazing animals can convert Vitamin K1 to Vitamin K2 (but as MK-4, not MK-7, the most bioavailable form of Vitamin K2.) Consequently, Vitamin K2 was no longer present in adequate amounts in common dietary staples, such as butter, eggs, cheese, and meat.

UK-based researcher CJ Prynne has noted that daily consumption of Vitamin K has decreased since 1950.[1] One reason is obvious: People are eating less leafy green vegetables, which are rich in Vitamin K1. Another reason is less obvious: The change in preparation practices also influences the low Vitamin K status. Traditionally, food was made in the presence of various bacteria species (synthesizing Vitamin K2), but international standards of food manufacturing have eliminated microorganisms, including beneficial flora, from multiplying and entering the human body.

How much do I have to eat to obtain Vitamin K2?

While MK-4 is often found in small amounts in meat and eggs, it is not sufficient and it is not MK-7. Vitamin K2 as MK-7 is also found in bacterially fermented foods like curd and mature cheeses. The problem is that we are frequently advised not to eat these foods because they can increase our cholesterol—and we would have to eat *a lot* to get only a little MK-7.

Research studies have suggested that 45 micrograms of Vitamin K2 is an adequate amount for children. However, for adults, up to 180 micrograms of Vitamin K2 has been shown to have beneficial effects. That number might actually be too low.[2]

In order to obtain just 45 micrograms of Vitamin K2 a day through diet, here are some examples of what you have to consume[3]:

Beef = 8 lbs. (4.4 kg)
Milk = 5 L (1.32 gal.)
Egg yolks = 8
Yogurt = 5 L

As you would agree, this is impractical and unreasonable. Besides, you are still not getting the *best form of Vitamin K2*—MK-7. You are consuming Vitamin K2 as MK-4, the less effective form of Vitamin K2.

MK-7 is rarely encountered in sufficient amounts in the Western diet. Again, the best source of that valuable form of Vitamin K2 is natto, the Japanese dish of fermented soybeans. Unfortunately, to most taste buds, natto—known for its questionable smell and slimy texture—is inedible. It is also very hard to find in supermarkets or restaurants.

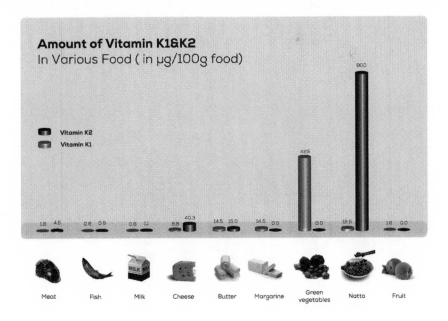

Amount of Vitamin K1&K2
In Various Food (in µg/100g food)

Vitamin K2
Vitamin K1

Are vegetables a good source of Vitamin K2?

Green, leafy vegetables such as spinach and kale, are in fact a source of Vitamin K, but Vitamin K1, not Vitamin K2. As previously discussed, Vitamin K1 is required for normal blood coagulation. Further, what Vitamin K1 is absorbed is utilized by the liver for the production of coagulation factors. It is not available for use by extra-hepatic tissues, such as the bones and the heart.

So do continue to consume your vegetables, but do not assume you are getting enough of the Vitamin K2 as MK-7 your body so desperately needs. That is why you need to supplement.

How do I find the right Vitamin K2 supplement?

There are a number of considerations for this question. First is dosage.

The recommended daily allowance (RDA) for Vitamin K1 is 80 to 120 micrograms. But there is currently no RDA for Vitamin K2. Research studies have found 180 micrograms of Vitamin K2 per day as a safe and effective dosage for adults. You will also want to make sure the supplement contains Vitamin K2 as MK-7. This may require a little research.

Healthy Hints:

4 Reasons You Might Not Get Enough Vitamin K2

1) Does your diet consist mostly of processed foods?

2) Do you only consume leafy greens for you vitamin K intake?

3) Have you just finished a long-term antibiotic therapy?

4) Do you suffer from chronic diarrhea and impaired gallbladder function?

If you have answered "yes" to any or all of these questions, your Vitamin K2 status is probably insufficient for the bone and heart benefits you should be getting.

The next consideration is what you might take with Vitamin K2. I recommend combination supplements that include Vitamin K2 with complementary nutrients such as vitamin D, calcium, and magnesium—all of which are necessary for optimal bone and heart health. This approach helps to simplify your nutritional supplement regimen, and is most cost-effective.

Finally, before starting any supplements, talk to your doctor. He or she may have a trusted supplement brand to recommend, and provide insight as to what might be most beneficial for your particular health goals. I will talk more about that crucial conversation—and the other healthy steps you must take—in the next, and final, chapter.

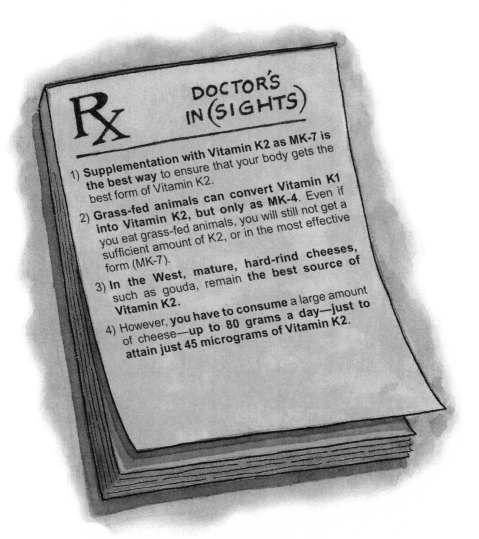

DOCTOR'S IN(SIGHTS)

1) **Supplementation with Vitamin K2 as MK-7 is the best way** to ensure that your body gets the best form of Vitamin K2.

2) **Grass-fed animals can convert Vitamin K1 into Vitamin K2, but only as MK-4.** Even if you eat grass-fed animals, you will still not get a sufficient amount of K2, or in the most effective form (MK-7).

3) **In the West, mature, hard-rind cheeses,** such as gouda, remain **the best source of Vitamin K2.**

4) However, **you have to consume** a large amount of cheese—**up to 80 grams a day—just to attain just 45 micrograms of Vitamin K2.**

NOTES

NOTES

Chapter 7

◄〇►

What Else Can I Do?

"Dr. Goodman, I'm convinced about Vitamin K2 and what it could possibly mean for my health. What else should I be doing?"

We are nearing the end of our talk about Vitamin K2, and I hope you have found it useful. Now, you have to continue that conversation with your physician.

You may have gotten a sense of the person behind the page. However, I do not know you as well as your doctor. I cannot answer your questions or offer advice tailored to your unique set of circumstances. I cannot direct you to specialists in your town.

Getting the most out of Vitamin K2 happens only if you make it is part of a personalized plan. That starts with talking to your doctor, someone who knows you best, with whom you feel comfortable. *This conversation needs to be candid*. It needs to go beyond determining the right amount of Vitamin K2 to take, but how to make it part of a healthy lifestyle. This cannot be stressed enough: This conversation is *essential*.

I believe your doctor and other health care practitioners are part of your team. But they cannot get healthy for you. Your good health and well-being depend on you.

What should I ask my doctor?

You should never be afraid to ask questions. In this case, knowledge is so much more than power, it is your guide to a healthier, more enjoyable future.

Two things to remember: First, *take down your doctor's answers* with a pen and pad or on your smartphone. Second, if you feel that your questions are not being *answered in a helpful manner*, find a doctor who will do so. (Even not knowing your doctor, I feel safe in saying that any physician would be delighted to have a patient who takes a proactive approach to his or her health.)

What should your discussion entail?[1]

- Discuss any symptoms you may have at the beginning of your visit.

- Ask, "Can we discuss my risk factors, and how to avoid diseases such as heart attacks, strokes, arthritis, dementia, cancer, and diabetes?"

- Your physician should talk to you about lifestyle changes involving nutrition, exercise and flexibility, stress management, and adequate sleep. Your doctor should have resources in all these areas.

- Ask, "What can I do to improve my current condition?"

- Your doctor may refer you to a nutritionist, personal trainer, or specialist for stress management and sleep disorders. The best advice I can give you is to take advantage of these referrals.

- Ask, "Given my current condition, what type of exercise, workout and flexibility routine should I be doing?"

- Ask, "Should I be taking any supplements and why?" (We have already discussed Vitamin K2 in detail in this book, so you'll be informed enough to discuss these options with your physicians.)

- Ask your doctor about any recent supplement research, which can be gleaned from the newsletters of reputable institutions such as Johns Hopkins, Harvard Medical, and New York University, which are available to all.

- Ask, "How should I be measuring my progress?"

- Ask, "When should I schedule a follow-up appointment?"

Healthy Hints:

How Do I Achieve A Healthy Lifestyle?

Earlier I talked about how exercise (walk whenever you can), diet (get away from acidic foods), and relaxation can benefit your overall health, including your heart and bones. Getting to the point where that becomes as normal as brushing your teeth is another matter entirely.

Patience is crucial. You see this at the beginning of every year. People flock to the gym and start diets only to give up hope before the Super Bowl. Expectations are unrealistic. People want to atone for a month of heavy eating with 30 minutes on the elliptical or some infomercial diet plan. Exercise and a proper diet are not fads. They need to be eased into, like a warm bath.

Find activities you like. There is no law that says you must join a gym to stay in shape. The most important thing is that you move your body. Perhaps you like gardening or a brisk walk. Maybe swimming gets you going. Find exercise that you love and stick to it. Look for opportunities in the flow of life: Take the stairs instead of the escalator. Park your car in the furthest spot of the parking lot and walk.

Adjusting to new foods requires time, ingenuity, and commitment. Remember, *you are not on a diet.* This is not about getting ready for swimsuit season or looking good for your 20-year reunion. You need to incorporate these healthier foods into your *life*, so find replacements, and make them gradually. For example, salmon burgers are a delicious alternative to hamburgers. A granola bar is a serviceable replacement for a candy bar. Mix cinnamon into your coffee, instead of adding sugar and cream. Remember: The more drastic the change you make—depriving yourself of carbohydrates or protein, for example—the harder you will fall when you slip. You are aiming for *consistency.*

Reducing stress is perhaps the hardest, because we tend to put ourselves last. To me, the solution is to put your version of stress relief—going for a walk, coffee with a friend, etc.—on your daily to-do list. You need to view that as an essential part of your day because it is.

Besides Vitamin K2, what other supplements are important?

As you know, Vitamin K2 is complementary to very important nutrients. It is a necessary addition to **calcium**, which is very beneficial, but comes with a potential significant downside: It can cause unwanted deposition of calcium in our arteries that can lead to blockages. Through its activation of the **matrix Gla protein (MGP)**, Vitamin K2 ultimately directs calcium to the bone, where it is needed, and away from the heart. Whether you are getting calcium through your diet or via a supplement, it is advisable to take Vitamin K2 as MK-7.

There are two other nutrients that I believe you should take with Vitamin K2. Again, you can discuss these (and additional) options with your doctor.

Vitamin D. Like Vitamin K2, vitamin D also works with calcium, by promoting calcium absorption in the gut and maintaining adequate serum calcium and phosphate concentrations to enable normal mineralization of bone and to prevent hypocalcemic tetany (i.e., spasms or cramps in the hands and feet).

Vitamin D is also needed for bone growth and bone remodeling by **osteoblasts** and **osteoclasts.**[2,3] Without sufficient vitamin D, bones can become thin, brittle, or misshapen. Vitamin D sufficiency prevents rickets in children and osteomalacia (softening of the bones) in adults.[2] With calcium, vitamin D also helps protect older adults from osteoporosis.[4]

Most importantly, vitamin D helps the body absorb calcium, while Vitamin K2 helps the body ensure that calcium is properly utilized (i.e., that it is ending up in the bones and not in the heart and blood vessels). Fortunately, it is very easy to measure vitamin D levels in the body and this helps to determine how much you need. Your doctor can test your vitamin D levels and offer insight about how it can be added to your routine.

Magnesium. Magnesium, like Vitamin K2, has a significant positive effect on bone and cardiovascular health. Hundreds of research studies confirm this, and you can read about this further in my book, *Magnificent Magnesium*.

Believe it or not, magnesium can help reduce the risk of heart disease by as much as 25 percent. With 80 percent of all Americans magnesium deficient, according to the World Health Organization (WHO), it is no coincidence that low magnesium levels are directly related to an increase in heart disease. Conversely, high magnesium levels are directly related to improved heart health. In fact, a 2010 article in the *American Journal of Clinical Nutrition* analyzed data of more than 88,000 women and found that those with the highest magnesium intake had a 37 percent lower risk of dying from sudden cardiac death.[5]

Magnesium is one of the most important minerals in our bodies. It is required for 350 enzyme systems, including converting ADP to ATP, the body's fuel supply (similar to the gas in your car). Simply put, we need ATP to create muscle action (including the beating of our hearts); we need magnesium to create ATP.[6,7]

Where can I get more information on Vitamin K2?

The International Science and Health Foundation, a non-profit research consortium, launched an information portal, VitaminK2.org,[8] in 2014. Created as a resource for consumers and practitioners alike, the site gets into the nuances of Vitamin K2 and features readable but in-depth summaries of the latest research on Vitamin K2's benefits.

You can also visit my website, <u>DennisGoodmanMD.com</u>,[9] for further discussion on Vitamin K2 as well as general health information. The research on Vitamin K2 is only going to grow, so I will do my best to keep you updated.

I cannot do the work for you, though. A healthy life is up to you. Supplements are only a small, but necessary, part of that. You have to do your best to eat a healthy diet, which includes no processed foods and no sugar. Exercise, stretch, and build up your muscles—ideally, every day. Stress management—think yoga, biofeedback, and meditation—is crucial, as is just taking time for yourself. Make sure you get enough sleep—at least eight hours a night.

No single element is enough. Each step in the right direction will keep you on the journey to wellness and a healthy life.

"Knowing is not enough; we must apply. Willing is not enough; we must do."
-- Johann Wolfgang von Goethe

In good health,
Dennis Goodman, MD

Healthy Hints:

What Do I Want You To Remember About Vitamin K2?

- New vital functions of Vitamin K—as Vitamin K2—have been discovered not related to blood clotting, specifically cardiovascular and bone health.

- In all cases, Vitamin K or K-related proteins play regulatory roles in important physiological processes.

- Vitamin K deficiency is widespread—even in healthy adults.

- No adverse effects of very high Vitamin K intake have been observed.

- To get the range of benefits that Vitamin K offers, you must take Vitamin K2 as MK-7 as a supplement. Food sources are limited, at best.

- I believe that further research is needed to conclusively prove that Vitamin K2 supplementation will result in a reduction of heart attack and stroke.

- In the meantime, I believe that there is enough evidence that supplementing with Vitamin K2 will help to improve your health, which in turn will enhance your quality and quantity of life.

℞ DOCTOR'S IN(SIGHTS)

1) **Vitamin K2 as MK-7** is an invaluable complementary supplement, especially with those that aid in bone and cardiovascular health such as **calcium, vitamin D, and magnesium**.

2) Before you start any supplementation program, please **consult your doctor.** He or she can determine the best course of action.

3) Vitamin K2 is **one part of a healthy lifestyle**. A balanced diet, exercise, stress management, and supplementation are equally important and must be done consistently.

4) **Achieving optimal health is up to you**.

NOTES

NOTES

Glossary

Absolute ucOC Test: measures the amount of osteocalcin not activated by Vitamin K2 in the blood, or uncarboxylated osteocalcin (ucOC) in the blood.

Absorption: the bone-building activity of osteoblasts.

Arterial Calcification: a state wherein arteries become rigid due to "cement" like layers of years of calcium deposits surrounding the inside of the artery; arterial calcification greatly restricts healthy blood flow to and from the heart.

Atherosclerosis: when the blood vessels become thick and stiff — sometimes restricting blood flow to your organs and tissues.

Calcium Paradox: although we need calcium, particularly for strong bones, it can potentially harm our cardiovascular system; Vitamin K2 is the answer to the calcium paradox.

Carboxylation: when a carbon atom double-bonded to an oxygen atom and single-bonded to a hydroxyl group is introduced. This lies behind Vitamin K2's bone and cardiovascular benefits.

Fermentation: the act of "aging" a food, allowing healthy bacteria to transform it. Natural vitamin K2 is the byproduct of such a process, which is why certain fermented cheeses are good sources of Vitamin K2.

Matrix Gla Protein (MGP): a protein that, when activated, helps ensure calcium in the bloodstream is not deposited into arteries.

Menaquinones: isomers characteristic of Vitamin K2; the length of the isomer side chains influences the availability to different tissues in the body; Vitamin K1's isomers are called **phylloquinones**.

Natto: a traditional Japanese breakfast food made with fermented soybeans; natto is the food that contains the richest source of natural Vitamin K2.

Osteoblasts: bone cells responsible for building up bone by a process called absorption.

Osteoclasts: bone cells responsible for breaking down bone by a process called resorption.

Osteocalcin: a protein found in bone and dentin responsible for regulating osteoclast activity; it's also the basis for the absolute ucOC test, which is how Vitamin K2 levels are measured.

Osteoporosis: a disease characterized by brittle, porous bone, caused by osteoclast activity that eclipses the activity of osteoblasts.

Remodeling: The process by which the entire skeleton is replaced every seven to 10 years through bone-building activity (absorption) and bone breakdown (resporption).

Resorption: the bone-destructive activity of the osteoclasts.

Endnotes

————◄○►————

Introduction

1. Knapen MHJ, Braam LAJL, Drummen NE, Bekers O, Hoeks APG, Vermeer C. Menaquinone-7 supplementation improves arterial stiffness in healthy postmenopausal women: double-blind randomised clinical trial. *Thromb Haemost* 2015 May: 0340-6245, http://th.schattauer.de/en/contents/archive/issue/special/manuscript/24032.html. Epub 2015 Feb 19.
2. The Centers for Disease Control and Prevention. "Heart Disease Facts." http://www.cdc.gov/heartdisease/facts.htm
3. *Ibid.* "Hip Fractures Among Older Americans." http://www.cdc.gov/HomeandRecreationalSafety/Falls/adulthipfx.html
4. Cummings SR, Black DM, Nevitt MC, Browner W, Cauley J, Ensrud K, Genant HK, Palermo L, Scott J, Vogt TM. "Study for Osteoporotic Fractures Research Group. Bone density at various sites for prediction of hip fractures." *Lancet* 1993 Jan 9,341(8837):72–5.

Chapter 1

1. Shearer MJ. 2003 in Physiology. Elsevier Sciences LTD. 6039-45.
2. Schurgers LJ, Teunissen KJ, Hamulyak K, Knapen MH, Vik H, Vermeer C., "Vitamin K-containing dietary supplements: comparison of synthetic vitamin K1 and natto-derived menaquinone-7." *Blood* 2007 Apr 15, 109(8):3279-83.
3. Kaneki M, Hedges SJ, Hosoi T, et al. "Japanese fermented soybean food as the major determinant of the large geographic difference

in circulating levels of vitamin K2; possible implications for hip-fracture risk." *Nutrition* 2001, 17(4):315-21.

4. Yaegashi Y, Onoda T, Tanno K, et al. "Association of hip fracture incidence and intake of calcium, magnesium, vitamin D, and vitamin K in Japan." *Eur J Epidemol* 2008, 23(3):219-25.

5. Stenflo J, Fernlund P, Egan W, Roepstorff P. "Vitamin K dependent modifications of glutamic acid residues in prothrombin." *Proc Natl Acad Sci USA* 1974, 71(7); 2730-3.

6. Nelsestuen GL, Zykovicz TH, Howard JB. "The mode of action of vitamin K. Identification of gamma-carboxyglutamic acid as a component of promthrombin." *J Biol Chem* 1974, 10;249(19);6347-50.

7. Rhéaume-Bleue, Kate. (2012). *Vitamin K2 and the Calcium Paradox: How a Little Known Vitamin Could Save Your Life*. Mississauga, Ontario. John Wiley & Sons Canada, Ltd.

8. Ikeda Y, Iki M., Morita A, et al. "Intake of fermented soybeans, natto, is associated with reduced bone loss in post menopausal women: Japanese population-based osteoporosis." *J Nutr* 2006, 136:1323-28.

9. Tsukamato Y, Ichise H, Kakuda H, et al. "Intake of fermented soybean (natto) increases circulating Vitamin K2 (menaquinone-7) and gamma-carboxylated osteocalcin concentration in normal individuals." *J Bone Miner Metab.* 2000, 18(4):216-22.

10. Eiji Monden: Natto lecture. 2007 Midwest Specialty Grain Conference & Trade Show. September 2007.

11. Annual report of Household Survey, Japan Bureau of Statistics.

Chapter 2

1. The American Heart Association. "Heart disease and stroke continue to threaten U.S. health." December 18, 2013. http://newsroom.heart.org/news/heart-disease-and-stroke-continue-to-threaten-u-s-health/

2. Ray KK, Seshasai SR, Erqou S, Sever P, Jukema JW, Ford I, Sattar N. "Statins and all-cause mortality in high-risk primary prevention: a meta-analysis of 11 randomized controlled trials

involving 65,229 participants." *Arch Intern Med.* 2010 Jun 28,170(12):1024-31. doi: 10.1001/archinternmed.2010.182.

3. WebMd. "Side Effects of Cholesterol-Lowering Statin Drugs." Reviewed by James Beckerman, MD, FACC. http://www.webmd.com/cholesterol-management/side-effects-of-statin-drugs?page=2#1

4. Shaw LJ, Raggi P, Berman DS, Callister TQ. "Coronary artery calcium as a measure of biologic age." *Atherosclerosis* 2006,188(1):112-9.

5. MedLine Plus, National Institutes of Health. "Heart Attack." http://www.nlm.nih.gov/medlineplus/heartattack.html

6. Luo G, Ducy P, McKee MD, Pinero GJ, Loyer E, Behringer RR, Karsenty G. "Spontaneous calcification of arteries and cartilage in mice lacking matrix GLA protein." *Nature* 1997, 386(6620):78-81.

7. Schurgers LJ, Cranenburg EC, Vermeer C.: "Matrix Gla-protein: The calcification inhibitor in need of vitamin K." *Thromb Haemost* 2008, 100:593-603.

8. Proudfoot D, Skepper JN, Shanahan CM, Weissberg PL. "Calcification of human vascular cells in vitro is correlated with high levels of matrix Gla protein and low levels of osteopontin expression." *Arterioscler Thromb Vasc Biol.* 1998, 18(3):379-88.

9. Spronk HM, Soute BA, Schurgers LJ, Cleutjens JP, Thijssen HH, De Mey JG, Vermeer C. "Matrix Gla protein accumulates at the border of regions of calcification and normal tissue in the media of the arterial vessel wall." *Biochem Biophys Res Commun.* 2001, 289(2):485-90.

10. Schurgers LJ, Dissel PE, Spronk HM, Soute BA, Dhore CR, Cleutjens JP, Vermeer C. "Role of vitamin K and vitamin K dependent proteins in vascular calcification." *Z Kardiol* 2001, 90: Suppl 3, 57-63.

11. Shearer MJ. 2003 in Physiology. Elsevier Sciences LTD. 6039-45.

12. Schurgers LJ, Teunissen KJ, Hamulyak K, Knapen MH, Vik H, Vermeer C., "Vitamin K-containing dietary supplements: comparison of synthetic vitamin K1 and natto-derived menaquinone-7." *Blood* 2007 Apr 15, 109(8):3279-83.

13. Cranenburg EC, Vermeer C, Koos R, et al. "The circulating inactive form of matrix Gla Protein (ucMGP) as a biomarker for cardiovascular calcification." *J Vasc Res.* 2008, 45(5):427-36.

14. Geleijnse JM, Vermeer C, Grobbee DE, Schurgers LJ, Knapen MH, van der Meer IM, Hofman A, Witteman JC.: "Dietary intake of menaquinone is associated with a reduced risk of coronary heart disease: the Rotterdam Study." *J Nutr.* 2004, 134(11):3100-5.

15. Gast GC, de Roos NM, Sluijs I, et al. "A high menaquinone intake reduces the incidence of coronary heart disease." *Nutr Metab Cardiovasc Dis.* 2009, 19:504-10.

16. Vitamin K.org. "Vitamin K Status Testing." http://vitamink2.org/k2-pedia/about-k2/

17. Rhéaume-Bleue, Kate. (2012). *Vitamin K2 and the Calcium Paradox: How a Little Known Vitamin Could Save Your Life.* Mississauga, Ontario. John Wiley & Sons Canada, Ltd.

18. Knapen MHJ, Braam LAJL, Drummen NE, Bekers O, Hoeks APG, Vermeer C. Menaquinone-7 supplementation improves arterial stiffness in healthy postmenopausal women: double-blind randomised clinical trial. *Thromb Haemost* 2015 May: 0340-6245, http://th.schattauer.de/en/contents/archive/issue/special/manuscript/24032.html. Epub 2015 Feb 19.

19. Scientific Opinion of the Panel on Dietetic Products, Nutrition, and Allergies. *The EFSA Journal* (2008), 822, 1-31.

20. Goodman, Dennis. (2014). *Magnificent Magnesium: Your Essential Key to A Healthy Heart & More.* Garden City Park, NY. Square One Publishers.

21. The Centers for Disease Control and Prevention. "Obesity and Overweight Data." http://www.cdc.gov/nchs/fastats/obesity-overweight.htm

Chapter 3

1. Johnell O and Kanis JA. "An estimate of the worldwide prevalence and disability associated with osteoporotic fractures." *Osteoporos Int.* 2006,17:1726.

2. EFFO and NOF. "Who are candidates for prevention and treatment for osteoporosis?" *Osteoporos Int.* 1997, 7:1.

3. Kanis JA. WHO Technical Report (2007), University of Sheffield, UK: 66.

4. Kennel KA, Drake MT. "Adverse Effects of Bisphosphonates: Implications for Osteoporosis Management." *Mayo Clin Proc.* Jul 2009, 84(7): 632-38.

5. Hart JP, Catterall A, Dodds RA, et al. "Circulating vitamin K1 levels in fractured neck of femur [letter]." *Lancet.* 1984, 2(8397):283.

6. Hodges SJ, Pilkington MJ, Stamp TC, Catterall A, Shearer MJ, Bitensky L, Chayen J. "Depressed levels of circulating menaquinones in patients with osteoporotic fractures of the spine and femoral neck." *Bone* 1991, 12:387-389.

7. Booth SL, Tucker KL, Chen H, Hannan MT, Gagnon DR, Cupples LA, Wilson PW, Ordovas J, Schaefer EJ, Dawson-Hughes B, Kiel DP. "Dietary vitamin K intakes are associated with hip fracture but not with bone mineral density in elderly men and women." *Am J Clin Nutr.* 2000, 71(5):1201-08.

8. Szulc P, Chapuy MC, Meunier PJ, Delmas PD. "Serum undercarboxylated osteocalcin is a marker of the risk of hip fracture in elderly women." *J Clin Invest.* 1993, 91(4):1769-1774.

9. Orimo, H, Shiraki, M, Tomita, A, Morii, H, Fujita, T and Ohata, M: "Effects of menatetrenone on the bone and calcium metabolism in osteoporosis: A double-blind placebo-controlled study." *J Bone Miner Metab* 1998,16:106-112.

10. Tsugawa N, Shiraki M, Suhara Y, Kamao M, Tanaka K, Okano T. "Vitamin K status of healthy Japanese women: age-related vitamin K requirement for gamma-carboxylation of osteocalcin." *Am J Clin Nutr.* 2006, 83(2):380-86.

11. Booth SL, Broe KE, Peterson JW, Cheng DM, Dawson-Hughes B, Gundberg CM, Cupples LA, Wilson PW, Kiel DP. "Associations between vitamin K biochemical measures and bone mineral density in men and women." *J Clin Endocrinol Metab.* 2004, 89(10):4904-09.

12. Knapen MH, Schurgers LJ, Vermeer C. "Vitamin K2 supplementation improves hip bone geometry and bone strength

indices in postmenopausal women." *Osteoporos Int.* 2007, 18(7):963-72.

13. Feskanich D, Weber P, Willett WC, Rockett H, Booth SL, Colditz GA. "Vitamin K intake and hip fractures in women: a prospective study." *Am J Clin Nutr.* 1999, 69(1):74-9.

14. Kaneki M, Hodges SJ, Hosoi T, Fujiwara S, Lyons A, Crean SJ, Ishida N, Nakagawa M, Takechi M, SanoY, Mizuno Y, Hoshino S, Miyao M, Inoue S, Horiki K, Shiraki M, Ouchi Y, Orimo H. "Japanese fermented soybean food as the major determinant of the large geographic difference in circulating levels of vitamin K2: possible implications for hip-fracture risk." *Nutrition* 2001, 17(4):315-21.

15. Ikeda Y, Iki M, Morita A, Kajita E, Kagamimori S, Kagawa Y, Yoneshima H. "Intake of fermented soybeans, natto, is associated with reduced bone loss in postmenopausal women: Japanese Population-Based Osteoporosis (JPOS) Study." *J Nutr.* 2006, 136(5):1323-28.

16. Knapen MH, Drummen NE, Smit E, Vermeer C, Theuwissen E. "Three-year low-dose menaquinone- 7 supplementation helps decrease bone loss in healthy postmenopausal women." *Osteoporos Int.* 2013 Sep, 24(9):2499-507.

17. Kanellakis **S,** Moschonis G, Tenta R, Schaafsma A, van den Heuvel EG, Papaioannou N, Lyritis G, Manios Y. "Changes in parameters of bone metabolism in postmenopausal women following a 12-month intervention period using dairy products enriched with calcium, vitamin D, and phylloquinone (vitamin K(1)) or menaquinone-7 (vitamin K (2)): the Postmenopausal Health Study II." *Calcif Tissue Int.* 2012 Apr, 90(4):251-62.

18. Yaegashi Y, Onoda T, Tanno K, Kuribayashi T, Sakata K, Orimo H. "Association of hip fracture incidence and intake of calcium, magnesium, vitamin D, and vitamin K." *Eur J Epidemiol.* 2008, 23(3):219-25.

19. Forli L, Bollerslev J, Simonsen S, et al. "Dietary vitamin K2 supplement improves bone status after lung and heart transplantation." *Transplantation* 2010, 89(4):458-64.

20. Rhéaume-Bleue, Kate. (2012). *Vitamin K2 and the Calcium Paradox: How a Little Known Vitamin Could Save Your Life.* Mississauga, Ontario. John Wiley & Sons Canada, Ltd.

21. UCSF Health Center. "Bone Density Scan." http://www. ucsfhealth.org/tests/001073.html

22. Jørgensen L, Joakimsen O, Rosvold Berntsen GK, Heuch I, Jacobsen BK. "Low bone mineral density is related to echogenic carotid artery plaques: a population-based study." *Am J Epidemiol.* 2004 Sep 15, 160(6):549-56.

23. Schulz E, Arfai K, Liu X, Sayre J, Gilsanz V. "Aortic calcification and the risk of osteoporosis and fractures." *J Clin Endocrin & Metabol* 2004, 89(9):4246-53.

24. Bostrom K, Watson KE, Horn S, et al. "Bone morphogenetic protein expression in human artherosclerotic lesons." *J Clin Invest* 1993 Apr, 91(4):1800-09.

25. den Uyl D, Nurmohamed MT, van Tuyl, LHD, Raterman, H, Lems, WF. "(Sub)clinical cardiovascular disease is associated with increased bone loss and fracture risk; a systematic review of the association between cardiovascular disease and osteoporosis." *Arthritis Research & Therapy* 2011, vol 13: R5.

Chapter 4

1. Edwards SL. "Maintaining calcium balance: physiology and implications." *Nurs Times* 2005, 101:58-61.

2. Xiao Q, Murphy RA, Houston DK, et al. "Dietary and supplemental calcium intake and cardiovascular disease mortality: the National Institutes of Health-AARP diet and health study." *JAMA Intern Med.* 2013, 173:639-46.

3. Bolland MJ, Grey A, Avenell A, et al. "Calcium supplements with or without vitamin D and risk of cardiovascular events: reanalysis of the Women's Health Initiative limited access dataset and meta-analysis." *BMJ* 2011, 342:d2040.

4. Pentti K, Tuppurainen MT, Honkanen R, et al. "Use of calcium supplements and the risk of coronary heart disease in 52-62-year-old women: The Kuopio Osteoporosis Risk Factor and Prevention Study." *Maturitas* 2009, 63:73-8.

5. Li K, Kaaks R, Linseisen J, et al. "Associations of dietary calcium intake and calcium supplementation with myocardial infarction and stroke risk and overall cardiovascular mortality in the Heidelberg cohort of the European Prospective Investigation into Cancer and Nutrition study (EPIC-Heidelberg)." *Heart* 2012;98: 920-5.

6. U.S. Department of Health and Human Services, National Kidney and Urologic Diseases Information Clearinghouse (NKUDIC). "Chronic Kidney Disease-Mineral and Bone Disorder." http://kidney.niddk.nih.gov/KUDiseases/pubs/CKD_Mineral_Bone/index.aspx

7. Goodman WG, Goldin J, Kuizon BD, et al. "Coronary-artery calcification in young adults with end-stage renal disease who are undergoing dialysis." *N Engl J Med.* 2000, 342:1478-83.

8. Russo D, Miranda I, Ruocco C, et al. "The progression of coronary artery calcification in predialysis patients on calcium carbonate or sevelamer." *Kidney Int.* 2007, 72:1255.

9. Jamal SA, Vandermeer B, Raggi P, et al. "Effect of calcium-based versus non-calcium-based phosphate binders on mortality in patients with chronic kidney disease: an updated systematic review and meta-analysis." *Lancet.* 2013.

10. Rhéaume-Bleue, Kate. (2012). *Vitamin K2 and the Calcium Paradox: How a Little Known Vitamin Could Save Your Life.* Mississauga, Ontario. John Wiley & Sons Canada, Ltd.

11. Geleijnse JM, Vermeer C, Grobbee DE, Schurgers LJ, Knapen MH, van der Meer IM, Hofman A, Witteman JC. "Dietary intake of menaquinone is associated with a reduced risk of coronary heart disease: the Rotterdam Study." *J Nutr.* 2004, 134(11):3100-5.

12. Knapen MH, Drummen NE, Smit E, Vermeer C, Theuwissen E. "Three-year low-dose menaquinone- 7 supplementation helps decrease bone loss in healthy postmenopausal women." *Osteoporos Int.* 2013 Sep, 24(9):2499-507.

13. Knapen MHJ, Braam LAJL, Drummen NE, Bekers O, Hoeks APG, Vermeer C. Menaquinone-7 supplementation improves arterial stiffness in healthy postmenopausal women: double-blind randomised clinical trial. *Thromb Haemost* 2015 May:

0340-6245, http://th.schattauer.de/en/contents/archive/issue/special/manuscript/24032.html. Epub 2015 Feb 19.

14. Committee to Review Dietary Reference Intakes for Vitamin D and Calcium, Food and Nutrition Board, Institute of Medicine. "Dietary Reference Intakes for Calcium and Vitamin D." Washington, DC: National Academy Press, 2010.

15. Bailey RL, Dodd KW, Goldman JA, et al. "Estimation of total usual calcium and vitamin D intakes in the United States." *J Nutr.* 2010, 140:817-22.

16. Dietary Reference Intakes for Calcium, Phosphorus, Magnesium, Vitamin D, and Fluoride Institute of Medicine (US) Standing Committee on the Scientific Evaluation of Dietary Reference Intakes. Washington (DC): National Academies Press (US); 1997.

Chapter 5

1. Greer FR. "Are breast-fed infants vitamin K deficient?" *Adv Exp Biol.* 2001, 501:391-5.

2. BabyCentre. "Vitamin K." http://www.babycentre.co.uk/a551938/vitamin-k

3. Beutler E, Lichtman MA, Coller BS. "Disorders of the vitamin K dependent coagulation factors." In: *Williams Hematology.* 5th ed. New York, NY: McGraw-Hill; 1995:1481-5.

4. Greer FR, Marshall S, Cherry J, Suttie JW. "Vitamin K status of lactating mothers, Human milk and breast-feeding infants." *Pediatr.* 1991, 88:751-6.

5. Cummings SR, Black DM, Nevitt MC, Browner W, Cauley J, Ensrud K, Genant HK, Palermo L, Scott J, Vogt TM. "Study for Osteoporotic Fractures Research Group. Bone density at various sites for prediction of hip fractures." *Lancet* 1993 Jan 9, 341(8837):72-5.

6. Theuwissen E., Magdeleyns E.J., Braam L.A.J.L., Teunissen K.J., Knapen M.H., Binnekamp I.A.G., van summeren M.J.H., Vermeer C. "Vitamin K status in healthy volunteers." *Food & Function* 2014, The Royal Society of Chemistry.

7. Prynne CJ, Thane CW, Prentice A, Wadsworth ME. "Intake and sources of phylloquinone (vitamin K(1)) in 4-year-old British

children: comparison between 1950 and the 1990s." *Public Health Nutr.* 2005 Apr, 8(2):171-80.

8. Khosla S, Melton LJ 3rd, Dekutoski MB, Achenbach SJ, Oberg AL, Riggs BL. "Incidence of childhood distal forearm fractures over 30 years: a population-based study." *JAMA.* 2003 Sep 17, 290(11):1479-85.

9. Kramhoft M, Bodtker S. "Epidemiology of distal forearm fractures in Danish children." *Acta Orthop Scand.* 1988 Oct, 59(5):557-9.

10. van Summeren M, Braam L, Noirt F, Kuis W, Vermeer C. "Pronounced elevation of undercarboxylated osteocalcin in healthy children." *Pediatr Res.* 2007 Mar, 61(3):366-70.

11. O'Connor E, Mølgaard C, Michaelsen KF, Jakobsen J, Lamberg-Allardt CJ, Cashman KD. "Serum percentage undercarboxylated osteocalcin, a sensitive measure of vitamin K status, and its relationship to bone health indices in Danish girls." *Br J Nutr.* 2007 Apr, 97(4):661-6.

12. Kalkwarf HJ, Khoury JC, Bean J, Elliot JG. "Vitamin K, bone turnover, and bone mass in girls." *Am J Clin Nutr.* 2004 Oct, 80(4):1075-80.

13. van Summeren MJ, Braam LA, Lilien MR, Schurgers LJ, Kuis W, Vermeer C. "The effect of menaquinone-7 (vitamin K2) supplementation on osteocalcin carboxylation in healthy prepubertal children." *Br J Nutr.* 2009 Oct, 102(8):1171-78.

14. Ozdemir MA, Yilmaz K, Abdulrezzak U, Muhtaroglu S, Patiroglu T, Karakukcu M, Unal E. "The efficacy of vitamin K2 and calcitriol combination on thalassemic osteopathy." *J Pediatr Hematol Oncol.* 2013 Nov, 35(8):623-7.

15. Ogawa, et al. "Toxicological studies of MK-4." *Pharmacometrics* 1971, 5(3):445-59.

16. Mikami, et al. "Study on the effect of MK-4 administered to rats during pre-and early gestational period and the pre-and postpartum period." Translated from Clinical report. 1981, 15(3):1143-59.

17. Goto, et al. "Study of MK-4 administered to rats during fetal organogenesis period." Translated from Clinical report. 1986, 20(11):7-38.

18. "Evaluation for safety of natto product named Kinnotsubu" (containing 13µg MK-7/g natto). http://hfnet.nih.go.jp/contents/detail405.html

19. Pucaj K, Rasmussen H, Møller M, Preston T. "Safety and toxicological evaluation of a synthetic vitamin K2, menaquinone-7." *Toxic. Mech. Methods* 2011, vol 21(7) p 520–532.

20. Beulens JWJ, Booth SL, van den Heuvel EGHM, Stoecklin E, Baka A, Vermeer C. "The role of menaquinones (vitamin K2) in human health." *Br J Nutr.* 2013, 110(08): 1357-68.

Chapter 6

1. Prynne CJ, Thane CW, Prentice A, Wadsworth ME. "Intake and sources of phylloquinone (vitamin K(1)) in 4-year-old British children: comparison between 1950 and the 1990s." *Public Health Nutr.* 2005, 8(2):171-80.

2. Beulens JWJ, Booth SL, van den Heuvel EGHM, Stoecklin E, Baka A, Vermeer C. "The role of menaquinones (vitamin K2) in human health." *Br J Nutr.* 2013, 110(08): 1357-68.

3. VitaminK2.org. "Adequate Intake & Dietary Sources." http://vitamink2.org/k2-pedia/about-k2/

Chapter 7

1. MedicineNet. "Questions to Ask Your Doctor." http://www.medicinenet.com/script/main/art.asp?articlekey=13683

2. Institute of Medicine, Food and Nutrition Board. Dietary Reference Intakes for Calcium and Vitamin D. Washington, DC: National Academy Press, 2010.

3. Cranney C, Horsely T, O'Donnell S, Weiler H, Ooi D, Atkinson S, et al. "Effectiveness and safety of vitamin D. Evidence Report/Technology Assessment No. 158," prepared by the University of Ottawa Evidence-based Practice Center under Contract No. 290-02.0021. AHRQ Publication No. 07-E013. Rockville, MD: Agency for Healthcare Research and Quality, 2007.

4. National Institutes of Health: Office of Dietary Supplements. "Vitamin D: Fact Sheet for Health Professionals." http://ods. od.nih.gov/factsheets/VitaminD-HealthProfessional/

5. Chiuve SE, Korngold EC, Januuzi Jr. JL, Gantzer ML, Albert CM. "Plasma and dietary magnesium and risk of sudden cardiac death in women." *Am J Clin Nutr.* First published November 24, 2010.

6. Goodman Dennis. "Magnesium: The Key to Heart Health." *Alternative Medicine* 2014 May/June, 28-29.

7. Goodman, Dennis. (2014). *Magnificent Magnesium: Your Essential Key to A Healthy Heart & More.* Garden City Park, NY. Square One Publishers.

8. VitaminK2.org

9. DennisGoodmanMD.com

74597504R00064

Made in the USA
Middletown, DE
27 May 2018